Lifestyle

English for work, socializing & travel

Pre-intermediate Workbook

John Sydes & Marie Kavanagh

PEARSON
Longman

Contents

1

A Present simple and continuous
B Present simple and adverbs of frequency
C **Communication strategies** Requests
D **Interaction** Networking

Building networks

A Present simple and continuous

1 🔊 **1** Listen to four people talking about their lives in another country and complete the table.

	Country he/she is from	**City he/she is living in at the moment**	**What he/she likes about the city they live in**	**What he/she doesn't like about the city they live in**	**Who he/she knows**
1 Christof	*Germany*				
2 Chandrika				*the weather*	*Jenny, Christof*
3 Jenny			*the shops*		
4 Chun Hua	*China*				

2 **Complete this text. Use the present simple or present continuous form of the verbs in brackets.**

It's 8:30 a.m. in New York and Christof [1] *is walking* (walk) to work. At the same time, Chandrika [2] ________ (work) on an important project with her team of IT specialists. She [3] ________ (call) a meeting three times a week to check progress.
It [4] ________ (rain) outside and Chandrika is happy she's in the office. Jenny [5] ________ (phone) home as often as possible. She [6] ________ (miss) her friends. Right now, she [7] ________ (fly) to Munich. It's 10:30 a.m. and Chun Hua [8] ________ (study) in the university library.

3 **Correct these sentences.**

1 Sam ~~is liking~~ *likes* London.
2 I listen to you. Please continue.
3 New York is having a lot of people.
4 I am driving to London every weekend.
5 Are you knowing Samantha?
6 John phones his mother right now so I can't ask him.
7 Are you wanting a cup of tea?
8 I'm not needing any help at the moment, thank you.

4 **Match words 1–6 with words/phrases a–f to form collocations.**

1	know	a	weight
2	drink	b	mistakes
3	belong to	c	a lot of people
4	make	d	Maths
5	study	e	mineral water
6	lose	f	a professional organization

5 **Complete these sentences. Use the collocations from exercise 4 in the correct form: present simple or present continuous.**

1 Mr Lee is from our Beijing office. He *knows a lot of people*. He thinks a big network is very important for business.
2 I'm a student at London University. I ________ because I want to be a Maths teacher.
3 I ________ every year when I train for the marathon. It's usually four or five kilos.
4 Sue only ________. She doesn't drink any tea or coffee.
5 It's normal in life to ________. The important thing is to learn from them.
6 I'm a teacher and I ________ of other teachers all over America. It's great for meeting people and getting new ideas.

B Present simple and adverbs of frequency

1 Complete this article about networking in China. Use one word from the box in each gap.

network successful acquaintances ~~relationship~~ contacts socializing people benefits

In China, business usually starts with developing a good [1] *relationship* with your business partners. This can be a slow process. It is important to have a strong [2]__________ of contacts with suppliers, banks, government officials and other business people. In China they call this *guanxi*. In the west, we describe a [3]__________ business person as rich; in China they describe this person as someone with a lot of [4]__________. There are many [5]__________ of *guanxi*: information; getting things done quickly and support in many areas. It is not easy to become part of a network and it can take a long time. It helps if you have friends and [6]__________ in the network and they can introduce you. Once you are in the network, you need to maintain your good connections by [7]__________ , giving small gifts and helping people.

Guanxi is about [8] __________ and not groups or companies so if you change your job, you take your connections with you. *Guanxi* is for life. It is possible for foreigners to become part of the network, but it may take longer.

2 Put the words in the correct order to make sentences.

1 always/fish/Friday./on/We/eat
We always eat fish on Friday.

2 you/doing?/are/What
____

3 work/Does/he/London?/in
____

4 morning./emails/every/check/normally/I/my
____

5 send/you/postcards?/usually/Do
____

6 time/get/morning?/What/Silvia/does/up/the/in
____

7 two/attend/I/every/year./conferences
____

8 English/Canada./am/studying/I/in
____

3 Complete these pairs of sentences. Put the frequency adverb in brackets in the correct place.

1 a John *sometimes* goes to conferences to get new business contacts. (sometimes).
b He doesn't remember names. (always)

2 a Americans change jobs several times in a lifetime. (often)
b They don't stay in the same town all their lives. (normally)

3 a I throw away business cards. (never)
b I don't remember to put them in a box. (usually)

4 a I go to social events because it's important to stay in touch with contacts. (frequently)
b I don't stay until the end of the event. (normally)

4 Complete this postcard. Use an appropriate adverb of frequency from the box in each gap

~~usually~~ never often rarely always sometimes

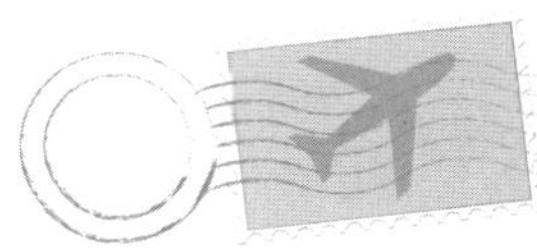

Hey Gerti!

You [1] *usually* (90%) *get a postcard from me from Brighton. You know I* [2]__________ (25%) *leave the UK, only if I have to. But here I am in Florida! It* [3] __________ (0%) *rains, and I* [4]__________ (75%) *lie on the beach all day and do nothing. It's great!*

You [5]__________ (100%) *say 'Try something new' so* [6]__________ (50%) *I do take your advice!*

Best wishes
Wilfi

1 Match requests a–e with the correct situations.

a Could you cover for me?

b Hi! Can you pick me up?

c Do you mind if I try it?

d Would you give me a hand?

e Do keep in touch.

1 You arrive very late by plane at the airport. There are no buses at this time. ▢

2 A good friend of yours is leaving to do an internship in Canada. You want to hear from him. ▢

3 You're moving house/ office. You need someone to help you. ▢

4 Your friend has a new digital camera. It looks very interesting. ▢

5 You want to take a longer lunch break. You ask your colleague if she could do your work. ▢

2 Match answers 1–6 with requests a–f.

1 Could I borrow your dictionary, please?

2 May I help you with your cases?

3 Do you mind if I take the last cookie?

4 Could you possibly pick me up at the hotel?

5 Do you think you could lend me $50?

6 Can you give me a lift into town?

a Of course. What time shall I come?

b I'd rather you didn't. I'm hungry!

c Sure. Here you are.

d OK. But when can you pay me back?

e I'm afraid not. I'm going in the other direction.

f That's OK. I can manage.

3 Look at replies a–f in exercise 2 again. Decide which replies are saying 'yes' (Y) and which are saying 'no' (N).

a (Y)

b ▢

c ▢

d ▢

e ▢

f ▢

4 Complete these requests. Choose the correct words/phrases.

1 *Do / Would* you like a cup of coffee?

2 *Do you mind helping / May you help* me with this translation?

3 *Could you tell / Tell* me the way to the station?

4 *Would you /Do you* like to have dinner with me this evening?

5 *Do / May* I carry your bags for you?

6 *Do you / May you* mind if I go early today?

5 2 Listen to the conversations and complete the answers to each request.

1 Sorry. I'm ________ I ________ it myself this evening. ▢

2 Please ________ ________. ▢

3 No, not ________ ________. Go ________. ▢

4 ________ free. ▢

5 Not ________ ________. ▢

6 Sure. ________ you ________. ▢

6 Listen again and decide if B is saying 'yes' (Y) or 'no' (N) to each request.

1 Put this conversation in the correct order.

- a Is this your first visit to the conference? ☐
- b Pleased to meet you, too. ☐
- c No, I came last year. May I give you my business card? ☐
- d It's a pleasure to meet you. [1]
- e Sure. Thanks. Here's mine. ☐
- f It is actually. And you? ☐

2 Read these notices and decide who can help each other. Complete the sentences.

1 Debbie and ________ can help each other.

2 Daniel and ________ can help each other.

I'm a busy, full-time music teacher with two small children. I have no time for hobbies and I'm studying again at university. Would like to swap piano lessons for baby-sitting three times a week.
Contact Debbie at DebRowe@t-online.com

Do you like fresh food? Would you like to eat more healthy foods? I'm planning to start a community vegetable garden. Do you want to join in? Of course you get free vegetables and plenty of fresh air in return for your help and the chance to meet people like you who want fresh products with no chemicals.
Email Daniel at Danielgarden@yahoo.com

I'm a retired person and new to the area. Unfortunately I have no relatives or friends here. I'm seeking an outdoor activity where I can be useful and meet new people. Who needs me? Edward, Edwardsmith@contact.de

My children are away at university and suddenly I have a lot of spare time. I have no hobbies to keep me busy. I want to work but I have no work experience. Does anyone need an experienced childminder? I would love to learn to play an instrument.
Please contact May, Maydunne@mailtoyou.com

3 Find words or expressions in the notices in Exercise 2 which mean the same as these words/phrases.

1 to exchange *swap*

2 get in touch ____________

3 have a lot to do ____________

4 neighbourhood ____________

5 take part in ____________

6 members of a family ____________

7 looking for ____________

8 person who looks after children ____________

4 Complete these email replies. Use the verbs in brackets in the correct form: present simple or present continuous.

1

Dear Debbie,

You 1________ (look for) a baby-sitter and I 2________ (try) to teach myself the piano. I 3________ (think) we can swap services! I 4________ (need) to do something with my time now my children are no longer at home.

5________ (you/want) references? Please contact me to arrange a meeting.

May

2

Dear Daniel,

I 6________ (like) the idea of a community garden.

Also I 7________ (want) to work outdoors and meet people.

My diet is simple. I 8________ (not eat) meat so the free vegetables are a bonus. I am very excited about taking part in your project. I look forward to your answer.

Eddie

2

A *will* for offers and decisions
B Emails
C **Communication strategies** Apologies
D **Interaction** Solving travel problems

Trouble-shooting

A *will* for offers and decisions

1 3 Listen to four conversations and decide if the statements are true (T) or false (F).

Conversation 1

1 Mr Willis cannot turn on his computer. (F)

2 Cathy Wong will connect Mr Willis to technical support. ☐

Conversation 2

3 Chris's computer has crashed three times this morning. ☐

4 Ken will have a meeting with the IT department to talk about the problem. ☐

Conversation 3

5 The help desk won't send someone to see what the problem is. ☐

6 The user wants to learn how to run the diagnostics test later. ☐

Conversation 4

7 Kate promises to send the file again. ☐

8 Becky will phone Kate if she has a problem opening the new file. ☐

2 4 Listen again and complete the first two conversations. Write one word in each gap.

1 C: Good morning, BRD Softlab. My name's Cathy. How can help you?
R: Oh, hello. My name's Richard Willis. I'm *having problems* installing a program, Money-Wise ...
C: Which version of Money-Wise do you use, Mr Willis?
R: The latest version, 8.0.
C: OK, Mr Willis. Just a moment. ________ ________ you ________ to technical support.

2 C: Oh no! Not again.
K: What's the matter, Chris?
C: The computer's ________ . It's the ________ time this morning and the last time it happened I lost an hour's work.
K: Really? How annoying. I'm going to the IT department for a meeting in a minute so I ________ ________ one of the technicians to ________ and ________ a look at your PC.

3 Match each problem 1–8 with the correct promise, decision or offer a–h.

Problem

1 Oh no! I've missed the bus to the airport. The next one's in an hour.

2 Oh dear. They don't take credit cards at this restaurant.

3 What will you do with all the money you won in the lottery?

4 Just look at that rain and I forgot my umbrella today.

5 Is Jack in the office today? I want to give him back the DVD he lent me.

6 What are we going to do about the problem?

7 Are you ready to order now?

8 I need the report at the end of next week.

Promise, decision or offer

a I think I'll stop working and buy a villa in Spain.

b No, he's not. Give it to me and I'll give it to him.

c That's OK. I'll pay. You can give me the money tomorrow.

d Yes, I'll have the steak.

e Don't worry. I'll give you a lift.

f No problem. I'll send it to you on Thursday.

g I don't know. I think I'll ask Ben to help me.

h I'll lend you mine. I don't need it. I came by car today.

1 Match phrases 1–8 with a phrase with a similar meaning a–h.

1 Hi Beth, [I]
2 For your information … [ ]
3 Thanks for your question about … [ ]
4 I'm attaching the information you requested. [ ]
5 Thank you. [ ]
6 I apologize for … [ ]
7 We're looking forward to seeing you. [ ]
8 Give me a call if anything's unclear. [ ]

a Re: your enquiry about … [ ]
b Cheers. [ ]
c I'm sorry about … [ ]
d Just to let you know … [ ]
e CU soon [ ]
f Dear Ms Granger, [ ]
g Please do not hesitate to contact me if you have any questions. [ ]
h Here's the file you wanted. [ ]

2 Look at the phrases in exercise 1 again and decide which ones are formal (F) and which are informal (I).

3 5 Listen and write the email and web addresses you hear.

1 ________________
2 ________________
3 ________________
4 ________________
5 ________________
6 ________________

4 Complete these sentences. Use a phrase from the box in each gap.

> I'm looking forward to … I'm waiting for …
> I'm expecting to …

1 ________ having a few days off work at the end of this month.
2 ________ Sally to tell me when and where the party is.
3 Paulo's coming back on Saturday. ________ seeing him again.
4 I sent the email yesterday evening, so ________ hear from them later today.
5 ________ see him when I'm in Berlin next month.
6 I can't speak Spanish so ________ her book to come out in English.
7 ________ meeting Sue Yates. She's coming to the meeting on Monday.
8 ________ them to send me the business cards I ordered.

5 Complete these extracts from emails. Use one word/phrase from the box in each gap.

> Thanks … Dear Mr … Hi … Love …
> Dear … Yours sincerely

1

________ Kate,
It was great to see you at the conference last week.

2

________ Ms Sousa,
Thank you for you order.

3

It would be great if you could let me have the report by Friday.
________,
Tom

4

We look forward to hearing from you.
____
Patricia Laker
Assistant manager

5

Anyway, it was lovely to see you and Carlos again. We must try to meet more often in future.
____
Sue x

6

________ and Mrs Fischer,
I am writing to confirm your reservation for a double room from 29th September.

1 Read this article about apologizing and decide if the statements are true (T) or false (F).

Saying you're sorry

Studies show that saying you are sorry is good for you because it can help to lower stress levels.

When should you say you're sorry?

It's important that you apologize if you do something wrong. The best way to apologize is to say you are sorry and/or …

- **a** accept that you are wrong.
- **b** explain why something happened.
- **c** promise that it will never happen again.
- **d** offer to do something that will help.

What should you do if you are both wrong?

In this case the best thing to do is to accept *you* are wrong and to say something like, 'I think we both made a mistake and I am sorry for the mistake I made'. If the other person doesn't accept your apology, you can still say you tried to do your best.

When shouldn't you say sorry?

You shouldn't say sorry if you don't think you did anything wrong and the mistake really wasn't your fault.

1 Saying sorry can be more stressful than not saying sorry. ▢

2 There is only one way to apologize and that is to promise you will not make that mistake again. ▢

3 You should say you are sorry if you make a mistake. ▢

4 If you make a mistake and someone else also makes a mistake, you should still say you are sorry for the mistake you made. ▢

5 If you say you are sorry but the other person doesn't accept your apology you can still say you tried to do your best. ▢

6 You should sometimes apologize even if something isn't your fault. ▢

2 Look at the article again and decide which of the four tips a–d are used in the apologies below.

1 I'm sorry I missed the meeting this morning. I had an urgent phone call from an important client. ▢

2 Oh, I'm sorry! Is that your coffee? Let me buy you another one. ▢

3 I'm sorry you didn't get the parts you ordered. John forgot to put your order into the system. ▢

4 I do apologize. I'll never do anything like that again. ▢

5 Oh dear! I'm terribly sorry. Please send me the bill and I'll pay for the damage. ▢

6 I'm sorry. That was my fault. ▢

7 Don't worry! I won't let it happen next time. ▢

8 I shouldn't have shouted at you. Please forgive me. ▢

3 Complete these conversations. Use one word/phrase from the box in each gap.

could you repeat that Please send me the bill we can't come to really must apologize ~~sorry I'm late~~ I'm sorry to bother you

1 A: I'm <u>*sorry I'm late*</u>. My train was delayed.
B: That's OK.

2 A: 0821 3335907
B: Sorry, ________?
A: Yes, that's 0821 3335907

3 A: That was a very mean thing to say, Jack.
B: Yes, I'm sorry. I ________ for what I said. It was stupid of me. I promise I'll never say anything like that again.

4 A: I'm afraid ________ your party on Saturday. Henry's mother is very ill so we're travelling up to Scotland to see her.
B: Oh that's a shame, but I understand.

5 A: Jane, ________. I need some help with the printer.
B: Oh, I'm afraid I'm busy right now. Can you wait 30 minutes?

6 A: Hey! Watch out! You just spilt soup on my jacket!
B: Oh, no! I'm terribly sorry. ________ and I'll pay for it.

1 Look at these things a traveller could say or hear and decide if you would hear them at a station (S), an airport (A), a hotel (H) or in a taxi (T).

1 I'm afraid I have to check out a day early. (H)
2 I'm not sure which terminal we have to go to. ( )
3 It leaves from platform 3 at 10:25. ( )
4 I need to get up at 5:30 so can you give me a wake-up call? ( )
5 I want to change some money. Can you stop at a bank? ( )
6 I'm afraid you'll have to check that other bag in. You can only take one piece of hand luggage on board. ( )
7 I'm afraid I can only take four people. ( )
8 I'd like a day return ticket please. ( )

2 6 Put this conversation in the correct order. Then listen and check.

OK, I'll come and pick you up. ( )
Its no trouble. I'll be in a red Mini. ( )
I'm still on the train, but I'll be at the station in 20 minutes. ( )
Hello Heinrich. Where are you? ( )
Oh thanks, Giuseppe. That's very kind of you. ( )
Looking forward to seeing you, too. ( )
Hi Giuseppe. It's Heinrich here. (1)
OK. Looking forward to seeing you. ( )

3 Find 21 words that are connected to travelling. They are written horizontally, vertically and diagonally.

R	X	T	E	R	M	I	N	A	L	Q
Y	O	S	U	I	T	C	A	S	E	J
Z	F	O	J	T	R	A	I	N	T	T
P	T	W	M	X	Z	Q	X	A	P	K
L	F	Q	A	I	S	L	E	I	A	Z
A	X	L	L	I	T	S	E	R	S	V
N	H	L	I	E	T	C	R	P	S	M
E	I	O	K	G	E	E	N	O	P	E
B	W	C	T	R	H	B	R	R	O	N
D	I	N	N	E	R	T	A	T	R	U
T	S	I	N	G	L	E	X	G	T	X

4 Which is the odd word in each group?

	a	b	c	d
1	**a** hand luggage	**b** bag	(**c** envelope)	**d** suitcase
2	**a** waitress	**b** cook	**c** manager	**d** guest
3	**a** the card	**b** the menu	**c** the order	**d** the bill
4	**a** presentation	**b** passenger	**c** conference	**d** speaker
5	**a** pilot	**b** immigration officer	**c** platform	**d** flight attendant
6	**a** receipt	**b** pay	**c** bill	**d** check in
7	**a** ticket	**b** cash	**c** credit card	**d** cheque
8	**a** passport	**b** duty free	**c** ticket	**d** boarding card

5 Complete these sentences. Use one word from exercise 4 in each gap.

1 Here's £30. Keep the change, but I need a *receipt*.
2 Which ________ does the train to Edinburgh leave from?
3 I'm afraid you can only take one piece of ________ onto the plane, you'll have to check one bag in.
4 Waiter, could we have the ________ please? Oh, and do you accept credit cards?
5 I'd like to buy some ________ perfume before we fly.
6 I have to give a ________ at a conference in Stockholm next month.
7 You have to show your passport and ________ before you can get on the plane.
8 The bus was almost empty. There was only me and one other ________ on it.

3

- **A** Past simple
- **B** Past simple questions
- **C** **Communication strategies** Active listening
- **D** **Interaction** Learning from experience

Roads to success

A Past simple

1 Write the past simple of these verbs.

present	past
1 go	*went*
2 run	________
3 sing	________
4 eat	________
5 drink	________
6 catch	________
7 leave	________
8 watch	________
9 write	________
10 work	________

2 Complete these sentences. Choose the correct form of the verb *be*.

1 It *was / were* really hot yesterday.

2 Jonny and Sam *was / were* at the party last night.

3 Alan *was / were* ill yesterday. He didn't go to work.

4 Our holiday *was / were* fantastic! I want to go again next year.

5 You *was / were* late for the meeting.

6 My boss *was / were* on a business trip yesterday.

7 Yesterday *wasn't / weren't* Monday.

8 We *wasn't / weren't* at home yesterday evening.

3 Complete this article about the pop singer, Michael Jackson. Write the past simple form of the verbs in brackets.

The Jackson

Michael Jackson, called the 'King of Pop', 1________ (become) one of the most successful singers of all time. He 2________ (be) born in Gary, Indiana in 1958 as one of nine children. He 3________ (die) at the age of 50 on June 25, 2009. Fans all over the world 4________ (be) sad and shocked that such a great artist was dead.

He 5________ (begin) his career as a singer with his brothers in 1964 in a group called *The Jackson 5*. In 1966 *The Jackson 5* 6________ (win) a local talent contest. The brothers 7________ (have) many successful songs, but, in 1971, Michael 8________ (decide) to start a career alone because he wanted to sing his own songs.

His 1982 album *Thriller* 9________ (be) an instant hit. It 10________ (sell) more than 100 million copies all over the world.

4 Complete these sentences about JK Rowling. Use the past simple form of the words in brackets.

1 JK Rowling ________ (be) born in Gloucestershire, England in 1965.

2 The idea for the Harry Potter story ________ (come) to her while she was on a delayed train to London.

3 After her mother ________ (die) in 1990, she ________ (not stay) in England. She ________ (go) to Portugal where she ________ (teach) English.

4 In Portugal she ________ (marry) a Portuguese man and ________ (have) a daughter.

5 Five years later, they ________ (come) back to Scotland where she ________ (give) up her teaching job to finish the first Harry Potter novel.

6 During this time she ________ (be) unemployed and ________ (not have) much money.

B Past simple questions

1 Look at the article about Michael Jackson on page 12 again. Then give short answers for these questions.

1 Was Michael Jackson called the 'King of Pop'?
Yes, he was.

2 Was Michael born in New York?
____

3 Were fans sad and shocked when he died?
____

4 Did he have ten brothers and sisters?
____

5 Was Michael's first band called *The Super 5s*?
____

6 Did *The Jackson 5* win a talent contest in 1966?
____

2 Reorder the words to make questions. Then give short answers.

1 to / Did / university / go / you?
Did you go to university? Yes, *I did*.

2 good / you / Were / a / student?
________ No, ________.

3 exams / pass / Did / your / you?
________ No, ________.

4 first / your / job / Was / interesting?
________ Yes, ________.

5 money / Did / much / you / earn?
________ No, ________.

6 nice / your / Were / colleagues?
________ Yes, ________.

3 Write the questions for these answers. Use the question words in the box.

How long	When	~~Where~~	What	Why	How much

1 *Where were you born?*
I was born in China.

2 ________
I left China in 2007.

3 ________
I left China because I went to university in London.

4 ________
I studied International Management.

5 ________
I stayed in London for five years.

6 ________
I didn't earn much money in my first job.

4 A friend set up his own business last year. Use the prompts to write questions you want to ask him.

1 Where/get/money?
Where did you get the money?

2 How much/money/need?
____

3 start/the business/alone?
____

4 How/get/the idea?
____

5 have/any problems?
____

6 What/business contacts/have?
____

7 lose/any money?
____

8 When/your company/become/a success?
____

5 One word in each of these sentences is incorrect. Find and correct them.

1 ~~Do~~ *Did* people enjoy the party last night?
2 I didn't went to the party.
3 Did John knew the answer?
4 He catched the plane on time.
5 Does the plane arrive on time yesterday?
6 We go on holiday last month.
7 Were it a good party last night?
8 Was Mike and Patty at school together?
9 Did Antje saw the film yesterday?
10 They finded the stolen car.

6 Complete these sentences with the correct form of the words *success* or *failure*.

1 Having a lot of business contacts is important for the *success* of a company.

2 Steve ________ his driving test the first time, but he passed it the second time.

3 To be a ________ business person, you must work hard.

4 Keep trying and you will ________!

5 My first company ended in total ________ because I didn't know enough about the business or the markets.

6 My last company was a great ________ and I earned a lot of money.

C Communication strategies Active listening

1 7 Listen to four conversations and complete these sentences.

1 A: I forgot where I parked my car!
B: ________ What did you do?
A: I spent more than 40 minutes looking for it.
B: ________! At least you found it.

2 A: I passed my driving test yesterday.
B: ________! ________! Was it your first test?
A: Yes, it was. And my Dad gave me his old car so I can go where I want now.
B: ________! … Actually, could you give me a lift into town?

3 A: You know I entered that singing competition? Well, I won it!
B: ________! ________! Were you on TV?
A: Yes, I was. Last Saturday.
B: ________! I missed it. ________.

4 A: Someone stole my laptop with my presentation on it.
B: ________. Did you get it back?
A: I'm afraid not. I had to write the presentation again, all those charts and slides.
B: ________. It must have taken a long time.

2 Look at the conversations in exercise 1 again. Which of the expressions are reacting to good news and which are reacting to bad news? Complete the table.

Reacting to good news	Reacting to bad news
	How terrible!

3 Match sentences 1–8 with an appropriate response a–h.

1 I lost my gold watch on the beach.
2 Three customers complained about our service yesterday.
3 I passed my final exams.
4 My boss gave me a pay rise.
5 Someone broke into my house and stole all my jewellery.
6 My first company was a disaster.
7 I got a £50 parking ticket in town yesterday.
8 I got the job I wanted.

a That's good news. How much did you get?
b How awful! Did you phone the police?
c Oh no! Did you find it again?
d Congratulations! When do you start work?
e Oh dear. I hope your next one was more successful.
f Well done! You must be very proud of yourself.
g You poor thing! Were all the car parks full?
h That's bad. Why were they dissatisfied?

4 Complete these conversations. Choose the correct responses.

1 A: Someone drove into my car this morning.
B: *That's terrible* / *Terrific!*

2 A: I didn't get the job I wanted.
B: *That's a pity. / That's fantastic.*

3 A: I lost my car keys in town.
B: *That's nice. / That's a nuisance.*

4 A: Our turnover last year increased by over 20 per cent!
B: *Oh no! / Wow!*

5 A: A customer cancelled a big order today.
B: *That's a shame. / Great.*

6 A: Our holiday was really good.
B: *Oh dear. / That's terrific.*

5 Develop this conversation. Use the words in brackets to write questions.

A: Hi Tim. 1 ________? (How/your holiday)
B: Hi Sam. Yes, it was quite good, thanks.
A: Oh good. 2 ________? (Where/go)
B: We went to Italy – to Rome and then Venice.
A: That sounds lovely. 3 ________? (weather/good)
B: Well, we had some sunny weather but it did rain quite a bit.
A: Oh dear, that's a shame. 4 ________? (food/good)
B: Yes, it was delicious! We ate lots of pasta and pizza – which I love!
A: Fantastic! I love Italian food, too. 5 ________? (enjoy/Rome)
B: Yes, it's a beautiful city. We saw lots of interesting places.
A: 6 ________? (visit/the Colosseum)
B: Yes, it was amazing! Have you been?
A: Oh yes, last year. It was incredible.

1 Match these sentence halves to make proverbs and quotes about success and failure.

1 Experience is the name
2 If at first you don't succeed
3 The only failure
4 Talk
5 Nothing succeeds
6 Genius is one per cent inspiration

a does not cook rice. (Chinese proverb)
b everybody gives to their mistakes. (Oscar Wilde)
c and 99 per cent perspiration*. (Thomas Edison)
d try, try again.
e is to give up trying.
f like success.

perspiration: a liquid produced by your body when you are hot and working hard. Also called *sweat*.

2 Complete this article. Write the past simple of the verbs in brackets.

Learning from mistakes

Thomas Edison 1 ________ (be) a successful businessman, but he also 2 ________ (make) a lot of mistakes. Before he 3 ________ (invent) the first light bulb, he 4 ________ (try) more than 6,000 times to get it right. But he 5 ________ (not stop) trying. When asked about his failures, he said, 'I 6 ________ (not fail). I discovered ten thousand ways which 7 ________ (not work)'. Failure is part of success, but only if you learn from it. Edison 8 ________ (learn) a lot from his experience.

3 Match verbs 1–8 with words/phrases a–h to form verb–noun collocations.

1 achieve	a the deadline
2 miss	b new machinery
3 speed up	c our targets
4 install	d tests
5 improve	e efficiency
6 run	f production
7 solve	g a lot of money
8 spend	h problems

4 Complete these sentences. Use the verb–noun collocations from exercise 3 in the past simple.

1 We ________ on new technology last year. It cost over a million pounds.

2 The new technology was a good investment. We ________ in all areas.

3 Our machinery and software were out-of-date so we ________ in the production area.

4 We ________ on the new machinery to make sure it worked.

5 The tests were not all good but we ________ very quickly.

6 The new technology was a success and we ________ by 20 per cent.

7 Unfortunately, we ________ of 1st December by about two months.

8 We improved efficiency and increased production so we ________. The production manager was very pleased.

5 Complete this email. Use the past simple of the verbs in brackets.

Subject: Installation of new machines

Dear Mr Summers

I'm sorry I 1 ________ (not get) back to you last week.
I 2 ________ (want) to wait for the results of our tests. As you know, we 3 ________ (miss) our deadline of the 19th July 2009 for installing five new machines.
We 4 ________ (run) some final tests on the machines. At first we 5 ________ (not find) the cause of the problem and then we 6 ________ (discover) what the problem was. Fortunately, we 7 ________ (solve) the problem yesterday.
Our new deadline is 25th August. Please let me know if this is convenient for you. I apologize once again for any problems we 8 ________ (cause) you.

Yours truly
Martha Hutchin

4

What's best?

A Comparative adjectives

1 Read this article about time and complete the sentences. Choose the correct answers.

The Speed of Life: Why time seems to speed up and how to slow it down

Is time going by faster or slower than it did when you were a child? Most people feel that the older they get, the faster time goes. The question is why?

Research shows that people feel that time is shorter now than it was when they were younger. One possible answer is the way we see time: a year is 1/10th of a ten-year-old child's life but only 1/50th of the life of a person who is 50.

Another theory is that the speed of time depends on how much information our minds absorb*. More information slows down time. Perhaps it explains why time goes so slowly for children. Their world is new and full of new information. Children live in a different world from adults – a more interesting and a more beautiful one.

absorb = to read or hear a large amount of new information and understand it

1 Older people think time goes past …
   a more slowly.
   b more quickly.
   c at the same speed.

2 One theory says that a year feels as if it is … longer to a ten-year-old that it does to a 50-year-old.
   a five times
   b ten times
   c 50 times

3 New information helps to make time go past more …
   a slowly.
   b quickly.
   c smoothly.

4 Children find the world more … than adults.
   a tiring
   b boring
   c interesting

2 Complete these tips about how to slow down time. Use the comparative form of the adjectives in brackets.

1 Don't do the same thing all the time – doing the same thing makes time go *faster* (fast).

2 Try to make your life ________ (interesting) by finding new things to do.

3 It is ________ (good) to go to different places than the same one when you go on holiday.

4 You can make your life feel (long) ________ by changing your job more often.

5 Try to see things in a fresh, new way. Try to be ________ (open).

6 Time doesn't have to go any ________ (quick) when you are 80 than when you are 18.

3 Look at the tips in exercise 2 again. Then look at the things Ian and Sue do and decide whether they help make their lives go by more quickly (Q) or more slowly (S).

1 Ian has moved house six times in the last ten years. (S)

2 Sue always spends her holidays at her parents' house in Scotland. ( )

3 Sue's hobby is cooking. Her favourite meal is roast lamb. She always cooks roast lamb on a Sunday. ( )

4 Ian loves travelling. This year he wants to go to Norway in the summer and Kenya in the winter. ( )

5 Sue is very active in an organization that helps homeless people and often travels around the country to visit the organization's homes. ( )

6 Ian's the assistant manager at a supermarket. He started there when he left school. ( )

B Comparative and superlative adjectives

1 Complete this table.

Adjective	Comparative	Superlative
small	1 *smaller*	the smallest
experienced	more experienced	2 ________
reliable	3 ________	the least reliable
happy	happier	4 ________
helpful	5 ________	the most helpful
6 ________	tidier	the tidiest
good	7 ________	the best
8 ________	worse	the worst

2 Complete these sentences. Use the superlatives of the adjectives in the box.

good popular ~~expensive~~ old big important

1 The world's *most expensive* book is Shakespeare's *First Folio*. Someone bought it for US$5.1million in 2006.

2 Ice skates were invented in Finland about 5,000 years ago, so ice skating is one of the ________ winter sports.

3 17 of America's 20 ________ hotels are in Las Vegas. The MGM Grand Hotel has 5,044 rooms.

4 Ts'ai Lun is one of the ________ people in history. He invented paper sometime between 100 and 150 AD.

5 Could this be the ________ job in the world? The Australian tourist board is looking for someone to work on a tropical island for six months of the year for a salary of £70,000.

6 Paris is one of the ________ tourist destinations in the world.

3 Complete these sentences. Use the comparative or superlative of the adjectives in brackets.

1 My brother gave me a pink and green tie for Christmas. It's the *worst* (bad) present I got.

2 £80 is too much for a gift. We need to find something which is ________ (expensive).

3 I think this card is much ________ (funny) than that one.

4 Do you think a book or a computer game is a ________ (good) present for a 12-year-old?

5 The ________ (unusual) present we got when we married was a goat

6 I think this ring is ________ (beautiful) and ________ (cheap) than that one.

7 Money isn't a problem, so what's the ________ (good) model you have?

8 My aunt usually gives me the ________ (awful) gifts. She gave me the ________ (ugly) hat I've ever seen for my birthday this year.

4 Read these statements and decide whether they are true (T) or false (F).

1 The Amazon River is the longest river in the world. It's about 500 km longer than the River Nile. ☐

2 A French woman, Jeanne Calment, is probably the oldest person to have ever lived. She died in 1997 at the age of 142. ☐

3 The biggest US state is Alaska. It's more than twice the size of the second biggest US state, Texas. ☐

4 The tallest tree in the world is over 100 metres high. ☐

5 The hottest temperature ever recorded was 61.2°C in Death Valley, USA. ☐

6 The deepest some whales can dive is about three kilometres. ☐

1 8 Look at the five situations a–e below. Then listen and match conversations 1–5 with situations a–e.

a giving a thank-you present for helping someone 2
b saying you like the way someone looks
c thanking someone for offering to help you do something you can't do
d saying you think someone has done something well
e helping someone out of a difficult situation

2 Listen again and complete the conversations.

1 A: I ________ your new hair style. It ________ ________.
B: Thanks, I'm glad you like it.
A: Yes, short hair ________ ________ you.

2 A: Here's a little something for all the help you've given us.
B: Oh, thank you, they're ________ but it really isn't ________.
A: Don't be silly! You're ________.

3 A: I ________ ________ your blog. It's full of useful information.
B: Oh, thanks. Sometimes I think my posts are a bit technical.
A: No, not ________ ________ – even I can understand them.

4 A: Oh no! I've forgotten the cable for the digital projector.
B: No ________. I've got one in my office. I'll get it.
A: Thanks, that's ________. You're a ________.

5 A: Just let us know what you need from the shops and we'll get it for you.
B: Thanks Mary, but are you ________? I don't want you to go to any trouble.
A: Don't be ________. It's no ________. It's only for a couple of weeks until you're well again.

3 Complete these thank-you messages. Use one word from the box in each gap.

lifesaver	conference	much	gift	Thanks	appreciate

Dear Sue,
Thank you so 1 ________ for my wonderful birthday present: the scarf and gloves are beautiful and they'll be very useful for the winter. It was a very generous 2 ________.
Thank you again.
Love,
Sam

Hi Bob,
Just a quick message to say thanks for your help organizing the 3 ________ yesterday. It was a great success and I really 4 ________ all your hard work.
Best regards,
Janet

Jim,
6 ________ for covering for me this afternoon.
You're a 5 ________!
Tom

4 Choose the best response in these situations.

1 Thanks for sending the information so quickly.
a You're welcome.
b I'm glad you like it.
c That's great.

2 Wow! You look fantastic in that new dress.
a Thanks, I know I do.
b Don't mention it.
c Thanks, I'm glad you like it.

3 You did a great job organizing the conference. Well done.
a Yes, I'm a fantastic organizer
b Thank you, it's very kind of you to say so.
c Are you sure?

4 These flowers are for you.
a Oh, they're lovely, but you didn't need to.
b Oh, I'm glad you bought some.
c Thanks, no problem.

5 I can pick David up on Saturday if you're busy.
a Don't mention it. I'm happy to help.
b That's very kind of you. Thanks.
c That's OK, you're welcome.

6 Don't worry. I'm sure I have a copy of that file on my laptop. I'll send it to you.
a Well done!
b Oh, it's wonderful.
c Thanks. You're a lifesaver.

7 The meal was absolutely delicious. You're a fantastic cook, Jane.
a Yes, I know I am.
b Oh thanks, Chris. I'm glad you enjoyed it.
c I'm not good at cooking.

8 I'm really looking forward to seeing you and Lucy again.
a Yes, so am I.
b You're welcome.
c Yes, we're really looking forward to seeing you, too.

9 I enjoyed your presentation – it was very interesting.
a Did you really?
b Thank you. I'm glad you found it interesting.
c Thanks. I thought so, too.

10 Thank you for my birthday present. It's great.
a You're welcome. I'm glad you like it.
b I'm glad you like it. It was very expensive.
c No problem.

1 Complete this crossword.

Across

1 Having a strong wish to do something and you will not let anyone stop you (10)

5 Allowing people to do, say or believe what they want without criticizing or punishing them (8)

6 Able to wait calmly for a long time or to accept difficult situations, etc. without becoming angry (7)

7 The opposite of stupid (11)

Down

1 Someone who steals or cheats and doesn't always tell the truth (9)

2 Someone who has a lot of energy (9)

3 Someone who thinks that good things will happen in the future (10)

4 The opposite of polite (8)

2 Complete these sentences. Use one word from the crossword in exercise 1 in each gap.

1 It doesn't matter how *energetic* and hard-working we are, there are usually more tasks than we can do so we have to prioritize and decide which tasks are more important.

2 Pete is one of the most ________ people I know. He speaks six or seven foreign languages and is interested in all kinds of things from architecture to classical music.

3 We have lost a lot of business recently and I'm not ________ that the situation will get better in the next few months.

4 In my country it is ________ to visit someone without giving them a small present like a box of chocolates or some flowers.

5 I'm not very ________; I don't like having to wait.

6 Benita lost her job because she was ________. She took photos of our new products and sold them to other companies.

7 Our new boss isn't very ________; she gets angry if we disagree with her.

8 Sam is very ________; he works hard and doesn't give up until he succeeds.

3 Complete this article. Use the comparative or superlative forms of the adjectives in brackets.

The 80:20 rule says that 80 per cent of what we do makes up for only 20 per cent of the value of our work. So we should put our time and energy into the 20 per cent of our work that adds the most value.

We sometimes don't have enough time or energy to do all the jobs we have so it is important that we prioritize. Prioritizing means deciding which jobs are the 1 *most important* (important) and are the ones we need to do first.

How do you decide if one job is 2 ________ (urgent) than another? The 3 ________ (good) way to prioritize jobs is to take a 4 ________ (close) look at them and ask which jobs are 5 ________ (important) than others.

Decide which jobs are the most important and 6 ________ (urgent) and classify them as your 'A' tasks. Your 'B' tasks are jobs that don't need doing immediately but are still important. All the other jobs, jobs that can wait until you have time, are the 'C' tasks. These are the 7 ________ (important) jobs.

Put your time and energy into doing your 'A' tasks first. Forget about your 'B' tasks until you have finished all your 'A' tasks. Then, when you don't have any more 'A' or 'B' tasks, you can start to work on your 'C' tasks.

5

- **A** *going to*
- **B** *will*
- **C** **Communication strategies** Offering help
- **D** **Interaction** Making plans

Organized chaos

A *going to*

1 Read this text about *Kaizen* and decide if the statements are true (T) or false (F).

Tim's workplace is not very efficient. But that is going to change. Tim isn't going to hire an expensive consultant to give him advice about what to change. He's going to introduce *Kaizen* which doesn't cost anything. *Kaizen* is a Japanese word: *kai* means change and *zen* means good. The theory is simple – make small changes regularly and you improve quality and efficiency. Most companies usually wait until they have problems and then make big changes.

Another Japanese word is *muda*, which means waste. When you identify *muda*, you can find ways to stop it. You can find examples of *muda* in most areas of a business, e.g. processes, time management, finances and raw materials.

At Tim's company, *Kaizen* isn't only going to involve top management – everyone is going to give examples of *muda*. Japanese companies such as Toyota and Cannon receive 60 to 70 examples of *muda* from each employee every year.

1 Tim's workplace is going to be more efficient in the future. ☐

2 Tim is going hire a consultant. ☐

3 The theory of *Kaizen* is complicated. ☐

4 Most companies make small changes when they have problems. ☐

5 *Muda* is a Japanese word for waste. ☐

6 *Kaizen* isn't going to involve everyone in Tim's company. ☐

2 9 Listen to three people a–c talking about *muda* and answer these questions.

Which person is talking about a waste of …

1 paper? ☐ 2 staff? ☐ 3 time? ☐

3 Listen again. Tick the things they are going to do to solve the problems.

A

1 limit the meetings to one hour ✓

2 limit the meetings to five people ☐

3 hold meetings standing up ☐

4 start meetings on time ☐

B

1 not send big email attachments ☐

2 have one file for all teams ☐

3 limit emails to five a day ☐

4 stop printing everything ☐

C

1 reduce the number of projects ☐

2 have one person to check all team and project work ☐

3 share information with all teams ☐

4 not have two teams working on the same project ☐

4 Complete these questions and answers. Use *going to* and the prompts in brackets.

1 A: We're having a lot of problems at the moment.
B: How *are we going to solve* (we, solve) them?
A: We ________ (hire) a consultant to help us.

2 A: The office is a mess.
B: When ________ (we, tidy) it?
A: We ________ (come) to work on Saturday and tidy it then.

3 A: My inbox is full.
B: What ________ (you, do) about it? I need to send you the report.
A: I ________ (delete) some emails this afternoon.

4 A: Our car got stolen.
B: Oh no! ________ (you, buy) a new one?
A: Yes, but we ________ (not spend) a lot of money.

5 A: I don't like my job. I want to leave the company.
B: Really? When ________ (you, quit)?
A: As soon as I can. I ________ (not do) another boring job again.

6 A: I was 65 last month.
B: Oh, really? When ________ (you, retire)?
A: Next year. I ________ (travel) around the world.

1 Rewrite these sentences. Use contracted forms.

1 It will be cold and wet tomorrow.

It'll be cold and wet tomorrow.

2 Most people will not stop learning in the future.

______

3 There will be more free time.

______

4 She will learn Chinese.

______

5 I will need to change my job several times.

______

6 We will not finish school before we're 18.

______

2 Complete these sentences. Use *will* and the verbs in brackets.

To do list

- *Finish the presentation*
  I [1] ______ *(contact) Sebastian this afternoon about the latest figures.*
- *Complete my tax forms*
  I [2] ______ *(fill in) the forms now and I* [3] ______ *(mail) them tomorrow.*
- *Emails*
  I [4] ______ *(deal with) the urgent ones first and I* [5] ______ *(delete) the unimportant ones at the same time.*
- *Book a hotel*
  I [6] ______ *(not put it off) any longer or we* [7] ______ *(find) one.*
- *Phone Sue*
  I [8] ______ *(not speak) for more than five minutes!*
- *Cancel tomorrow's meeting*
  I [9] ______ *(rearrange) for next week when I have more time.*
- *Check tomorrow's plan*
  I [10] ______ *(send) an email and confirm the times.*

3 Rewrite these sentences to ask questions about the future using *will*. Then give short answers.

1 Lifelong learning will be important for everyone.

A: *Will lifelong learning be important for everyone?*

B: *Yes, it will.*

2 Most people will retire earlier.

A: ______?

B: No, ______

3 Employees will need more skills.

A: ______?

B: Yes, ______

4 English will be a second language for most people.

A: ______?

B: Yes, ______

5 Multi-tasking will increase productivity.

A: ______?

B: No, ______

6 Children will spend less time at school.

A: ______?

B: No, ______

4 Match sentences halves 1–6 with a–f.

1 He's going to retire next year

2 I'll phone you tomorrow

3 I want to lose ten kilograms this year

4 Air travel will probably be much cheaper

5 I can't meet you this afternoon

6 Students won't use books in the future

a to arrange a time and place for the meeting.

b in 20 years' time.

c and travel around the world.

d because I'm going to meet Sam for a coffee.

e they'll use computers instead.

f so I'm going to join a gym next week.

5 Complete these sentences. Use *going to* or *will* and a verb from the box in each gap.

introduce	not rain	~~study~~	not pass	arrange	not pay off

1 I want to learn a new language so *I'm going to study* Chinese next year.

2 Please email me the details and I ______ the meeting for you.

3 Harry ______ his exams because he never studies.

4 We ______ some changes that will increase productivity.

5 I ______ my debts this month because I can't afford it.

6 The weather report said that it ______ today so let's go to the beach!

C Communication strategies | Offering help

1 Put these words into the correct order to make requests.

1 me/$10/you/Can/lend?

____?

2 mind/you/if/Do/the/window/open/I?

____?

3 me/up/Could/pick/you/4 p.m./at?

____?

4 get/Would/a/you/me/glass of water?

____?

5 a/give/me/you/hand/Can?

____?

6 borrow/I/your/May/calculator?

____?

2 Match indirect requests 1–6 with direct requests a–f.

1 That cake looks nice.
2 I can't concentrate
3 Your desk is full of old papers.
4 Are you going shopping?
5 This bottle is difficult to open.
6 I forgot to bring my dictionary.

a Would you buy me a pint of milk?
b Can I have a piece?
c May I borrow yours?
d Could you turn the music down?
e Could you please tidy it?
f Can you open it for me?

3 Match requests 1–10 with responses a–j.

1 It's rather warm in here.
2 Is anyone going to the station?
3 These suitcases are really heavy.
4 Can I hang my coat up here?
5 I can't read the report.
6 I'm having a lot of problems with this presentation.
7 Do you mind if I borrow your dictionary?
8 I'm quite thirsty.
9 May I use your mobile phone?
10 Would you copy this for me?

a Can I carry them for you?
b Yes. Would you like a lift?
c Sorry. I'm afraid the battery has run out.
d Sure. May I take your coat for you?
e No problem. How many copies do you want?
f Would you like something to drink?
g Shall I open the window?
h Would you like some help with it? Perhaps I could make some suggestions.
i Not at all. Here you are.
j Shall I put the light on?

4 Look at requests 1–10 in exercise 3 again. Decide which are direct (D) and which are indirect (I).

5 10 Listen to four conversations. Decide which requests are direct (D) and which are indirect (I).

1 ☐
2 ☐
3 ☐
4 ☐

6 Listen again and complete these sentences.

1 A: Do you think I ________ ________ your car?
B: I'm ________ not. …
A: No ________. I'll take the bus.

2 A: I've got my English test tomorrow and I can't find my ________ anywhere.
B: ________ ________ ________ to take mine?
A: That ________ ________ great. …

3 A: … ________ you ________ to stay for dinner?
B: I don't want to be any ________.

4 A: ________ you ________ me with this email? I don't know what to write.
B: Yes, ________ ________. Just give me a minute and I'll be right with you.

7 Complete this email. Use one word from the box in each gap.

easiest How could OK why happy

Hi Kim,

Thanks for your email. The job sounds very interesting. I'd be [1] ________ to help you with your CV. [2] ________ about meeting up some time this week to talk about it? Is Thursday evening [3] ________ for you? If that's not convenient, [4] ________ don't you email me your CV? – I [5] ________ send it back to you before the weekend.
Let me know what's [6] ________ for you.

Best,
Tracy

1 Complete this article. Use one word from the box in each gap.

managing run put off deal with waste effectively

How organized are you?

Are you well-organized and good at 1__________ your time? If so, you don't need to 2__________ your time reading this article about time management. Stop here. But if you often find you 3 __________ out of time and 4 __________ doing important tasks until the last minute, then read on, because you don't know how to manage your time 5__________.

A very simple tool in time management is a To-Do list. You write the most important task you have to 6 __________ at the top and the least important at the bottom. Then just work your way through the list. But remember: you can't change the order of the tasks …

2 Match sentence halves 1–6 with a–f to make correct sentences.

1 John put off cleaning his windows for so long,
2 Don't put off changing your tyres
3 I never put off going to the dentist
4 I'm going to put off doing my taxes
5 I can't put off talking to my mother
6 I put off checking my emails on Mondays

a because I want to keep my teeth healthy.
b until my accountant sends me the forms.
c because she phones me every week!
d he couldn't see out of them.
e because there are always more than a hundred after the weekend.
f because it's going to snow next week.

3 Complete this puzzle and find the hidden word.

Clues

1 If you ask someone to do something, you make a …
2 Not the same
3 The opposite of the past
4 Doing more than one thing at a time
5 If a tax form, for example, is not easy to understand, it's …
6 Another word for *employ* someone
7 When something is very untidy, it's a …
8 A person who keeps records of how much money a business or person has
9 When you delay something because you don't want to do it

6

A Numbers
B Question forms
C **Communication strategies** Persuasion
D **Interaction** A sales presentation

Features and benefits

A Numbers

1 Read this article about a high-tech toy. Then complete the table of specifications.

WowWee FlyTech Dragonfly

This flying *bug** is not just a toy for kids – I had just as much fun flying it as my ten-year-old son. The 28 gram toy flies by flapping its wings up and down just like a real dragonfly. It has a top speed of about 30 km/h so you need a large room if you want to fly it indoors. It is bigger than I expected – it's 31.2 cm long, 8.6 cm high and the wings are 42 cm wide.

The control unit needs six AA batteries, which are not included. The control unit is also used to charge the toy's internal battery. It takes about 20 minutes to charge the bug and when fully-charged it can fly for between five to ten minutes. The control unit has two channels: one to control the wings and one to control the tail, it also has two skills levels: beginner and advanced. I'm still at the beginner level but after a few flights my son had no problem flying the bug at the advanced level.

When we tested the bug outside, we soon found that it is impossible to fly when the wind is stronger than about five km/h. We also found that we lost control of the bug when it flew more than about 15 metres from the control unit.

The bug retails in the shops for about US$ 40. We had a lot of fun with the bug and think it is worth every cent.

bug = an insect

Specifications	WowWee Flytech Dragonfly
1 *Length*	32.1 cm
Height	2 ________
3 ________	42 cm
4 ________	28 g
Batteries	5 ________ AA (not included)
6 ________	30 km/h
Battery charging time	7 ________
8 ________	US $40

2 Look at the article again and complete these sentences. Choose the correct answers.

1 The bug is for …
a kids. b adults. c kids and adults.

2 The bug's wings are … its body.
a shorter than b longer than c the same length as

3 The writer found the bug … to fly … his son.
a easier … than b more difficult … than c as difficult … as

3 Write these numbers as you would say them.

1 2.185 *two point one, eight, five*
2 ¾ ________
3 500,050 ________
4 €14.95 ________
5 2,185 ________
6 550,000 ________
7 089-3147-9261 ________
8 12,850,000 ________
9 967.254 ________
10 ☎ 08551-411179 ________

B Question forms

1 Complete the table with the missing adjectives and nouns.

Adjective	Noun
heavy	weight
high	2 ______
wide	3 ______
4 ______	length
deep	5 ______
6 ______	speed

2 11 Listen to a conversation between a car salesman and a customer and decide if the statements are true (T) or false (F).

1 The Aptera weighs the same as a normal car. ☐
2 The Aptera's top speed is 180 miles per hour. ☐
3 The Aptera runs on gas and electricity. ☐
4 The Aptera doesn't need any gas for journeys less than 50 miles. ☐
5 One of the companies investing in Aptera Motors is Google. ☐
6 The Aptera costs $50,000. ☐

3 You would like to find out more about the Aptera 2h. Look at these answers and write the questions.

1 ______ *How long is it* ______?
It's 439 cm long.

2 ______________________?
It's 231 cm wide.

3 ______________________?
It weighs 670 kg.

4 ______________________?
The top speed is 136km/h.

5 ______________________?
The electric engine can produce 30 kW of power.

6 ______________________?
It only costs US$ 29,900.

4 Read this blog about an electronic dictionary and answer the questions.

This electronic dictionary has to be my favourite gadget. It's light and small and easily fits into a bag or your pocket. The display is large (83 x 44 mm) and shows ten lines of text. I was amazed at how many words it translates, it only weighs 190 grams, but it has over five million entries in it.

Another great thing about it is you can download lots of different language dictionaries. I have to work a lot with German speakers, so it's ideal for me because the standard dictionary is German–English, English–German. However, last month I had to fly to Madrid for a week, so I downloaded a Spanish–English, English–Spanish dictionary onto an SD card (which you have to buy separately). I didn't need it much in my meetings with my Spanish colleagues because they all spoke very good English, but it was really useful in the evenings when I was in a café or restaurant and the staff didn't speak English.

It is quite expensive – I paid $249 for mine – but if you often travel to other countries on business it's worth every penny.

1 How wide is the display?
83mm

2 What's the height of the display?
____

3 How heavy is the dictionary?
____

4 How many definitions does the dictionary have?
____

5 Does the dictionary come with an SD card?
____

6 How much does the dictionary cost?
____

C Communication strategies | Persuasion

1 Read these phrases used by salespeople and decide what kind of product they are trying to persuade someone to buy.

1 The price includes software, a 4GB memory card and a carrying case.

a a flat screen TV **b** a digital camera **c** a book

2 Wow, it makes you look about ten years younger. You look fantastic in it.

a a handbag **b** sunglasses **c** a dress

3 Just imagine what your neighbours will say when they see it parked outside your house.

a a new car **b** a new suit **c** a new hair cut

4 If you sign a two-year contract, we won't charge you for any local calls you make in the first three months.

a a mobile phone **b** business cards **c** a credit card

5 Book your ticket now! This offer ends on 15th August.

a a telephone **b** a newspaper **c** a flight

6 The lite version of our program costs €159, but for just €199 you can now buy the premium version with six months free technical support.

a a flat screen TV **b** software **c** a watch

3 🔊 **12** Listen to a second-hand-car salesman talking to some customers. Which sales techniques from exercise 2 does he use?

4 🔊 Listen again and complete the conversation. Write one word in each gap.

A: Good afternoon, madam. Can I help you?

B: Yes, I'd like to know a ________ ________ ________ the red car out there.

A: Ah, the Golf? Well, it's only had one careful ________ and no ________.

B: Yes, it looks as if it's in very good ________.

A: Yes, there's nothing wrong with that car. I'm ________ it with a two-year guarantee.

B: Really?

A: Yes, there's been a lot of interest in that car, so if you're thinking of buying it, don't think too long because I ________ ________ that it'll still be for sale tomorrow.

B: OK and you want £12,000 for it?

2 Which sales techniques are these salespeople using? Match items 1–6 with sales techniques a–f.

1 ☐
Buy now! ▶ **Don't miss this fantastic opportunity. Remember this special offer is only for orders received before 31st May.**

2 ☐
Paris has never been so cheap! Flights from as little as €49.95*
** The price does not include airport taxes, or fuel.*

3 ☐
If you buy the cooker, we'll include four cooking pots, a frying pan and six cookery books.

4 ☐
I can tell you're an expert in this area, madam. It's a pleasure to talk to someone who really understands digital photography. I'm sure you'll be impressed with this new model.

5 ☐
It's cheaper, lighter and stronger than other models in its class.

6 ☐
When would be the best time to install the satellite dish and would you like us to remove your old TV aerial?

a List your products features or benefits in threes.

b Offer a fantastic price.

c Assume your customer is going to buy your product.

d Give things away.

e Say there aren't many products left or they're only available for a limited time.

f Pay your customer compliments and flatter them.

D Interaction A sales presentation

1 Complete these sentences about some products' features and benefits. Add *-able* or *-ful* to the words in brackets.

1 You won't find a more *comfortable* (comfort) office chair than the Ergosit.

2 The special filter removes any ________ (harm) bacteria from the water and guarantees it is safe to drink.

3 I can recommend the company PC Doctors. They are friendly, ________ (rely) and professional.

4 This is a ________ (wonder) film about the planet Earth and the photography is (beauty) ________.

5 If you are looking for a ________ (fashion), modern watch, visit our store – we have more than 2,000 different models to choose from.

6 Our houses are ________ (afford) and built using energy saving materials.

2 Decide if these statements are about a product's features (F) or its benefits (B).

1 It is powered by three AAA batteries. (F)

2 It's simple and great fun to use. ( )

3 You only need to use it for five minutes every day to stay fit and healthy. ( )

4 There are six different models to choose from. ( )

5 It's environmentally friendly and you can recycle it. ( )

6 It's made of steel and aluminium and weighs 9.5 kg. ( )

7 It's the perfect way to learn a foreign language quickly and easily. ( )

8 It's small enough to fit inside your pocket. ( )

9 The touch screen measures 60 mm x 90 mm and displays all the phone's features. ( )

10 The easy and healthy way to lose weight. ( )

3 These extracts from a product presentation are in the wrong order. Put them in the correct order.

A ( )
Our Quest III solar panels work even when they are not in direct sunlight. This means they can be used on any building and in places which do not get many days sunshine a year, London or New York, for example. The panels are extremely light, which means you can fit them on roofs without having to reinforce* or strengthen* them.

B ( )
Now as you all know, you normally have to install solar panels so that they point at the sun and to work best they need to be at 45° to the sun. This means that the roofs of a lot of buildings cannot be fitted with solar panels because they do not face south, but east-west.

C ( )
Good morning, everyone. Thank you for coming. My name's Julie Finch and I'm the sales manager for SolarQuest, a company that produces solar panels. Today I'd like to tell you about our latest panels, Quest III.

D ( )
Now, if there are any questions, I'd be more than happy to try and answer them.

E ( )
So, to sum up, our Quest III panels are lightweight, can be installed anywhere and the installation is simple and cheap.

reinforce, strengthen = to make something stronger

A solar panel

7

A Modals of obligation
B Modal question forms
C **Communication strategies** Instructions
D **Interaction** Learning from play

Playing by the rules

A Modals of obligation

1 What do the modal verbs in these sentences mean? Match the sentences with the correct definitions.

1 You *mustn't* drop litter in the street in Singapore.

2 You *shouldn't* wrap presents in white paper in China.

3 You *have to* drive with your lights on during the day in Italy.

4 You *don't have to* eat with chopsticks in Japan.

5 You *should* hand over your business card with two hands in China.

6 You *can* wear jeans to work on casual Friday in the US.

a a good idea or the right thing to do

b not necessary

c forbidden or not allowed

d not a good idea or the wrong thing to do

e necessary or obligatory

f possible or allowed

2 Complete these sentences. Choose the correct modal verbs.

1 You *must / needn't* fasten your seatbelt when the plane is taking off.

2 You *mustn't / don't need to* smoke in public buildings in Ireland.

3 Employees *needn't / mustn't* use the office phone to make personal calls.

4 Visitors from the European Union *don't need to / shouldn't* have a visa to enter the UK.

5 You *don't need to / should* save a file before you turn off the computer, or you will lose it.

6 You *have to / mustn't* pay income tax in France.

7 If you want a driving license in the US you *must / shouldn't* be over 16 years of age.

8 Children *have to / mustn't* go to school in most countries.

3 13 Listen to a consultant giving advice about living and working in Germany and decide if these sentences are true (T) or false (F)?

1 At work, you may use colleagues' first names immediately.

2 People needn't wear uniforms at work.

3 People must come to meetings on time.

4 You can use your mobile phone in meetings.

5 You needn't book a table in popular restaurants

6 You can drive faster than 90 kilometres on motorways.

7 You have to wear a seat belt when driving.

8 You can wash your car any day of the week.

4 Complete this puzzle to find the hidden word

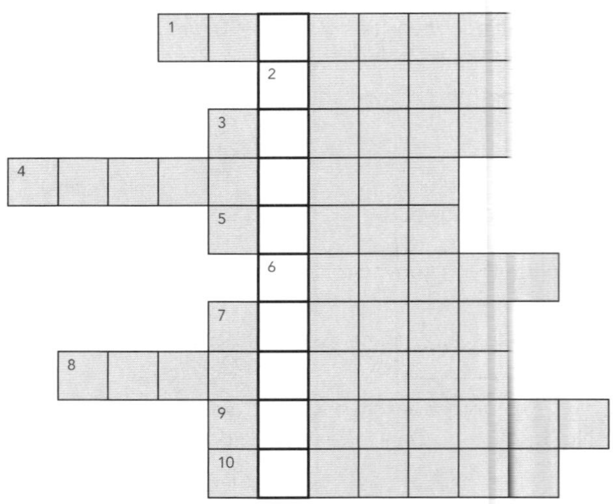

Clues

1 Make better

2 You need to do this after a hard day at work

3 The positive feeling people have about their work

4 To bring in something new, a dress code for example

5 You must obey these in the workplace.

6 People feel very comfortable wearing these clothes.

7 You feel this if you work under a lot of pressure.

8 The opposite of easy

9 This means not just one person but all the people.

10 If something is good for you, it is a …

1 Match these sentence halves to make correct sentences.

1 Can you work
2 You needn't
3 Do you have
4 You mustn't
5 You must
6 Should I

a make private phone calls at work.
b quit my job and find a new one?
c to wear a uniform at work?
d from home whenever you want?
e go shopping. I bought everything we need yesterday.
f fasten your seat belt when you are driving in the car.

2 Complete these conversations. Re–order the words in brackets to make questions

1 A: ________________________? (you/jeans/at/work/Can/wear)
B: No. I can't. I have to wear a suit and tie.

2 A: ________________________? (have to/you/Do/be at/work/before 9 a.m.)
B: No, I don't. I start work at 9:30.

3 A: ________________________? (the report/I/send/have to/today/Do)
B: No, you don't .Tomorrow will be fine.

4 A: I want to leave the office early today.
________________________? (ask/I/for permission/Do/need to)
B: Yes, you do.

5 A: ________________________? (in meetings/we/switch off/Should/our mobile phones)
B: Yes, of course.

6 A: ________________________? (private calls/in the office/Can/make/you)
B: No, it's not allowed.

3 Complete these conversations. Write one word in each gap.

1 A: It's hot in here. *Can* I open the window?
B: No, you ________. It's not allowed.

2 A: ________ you have to work on Saturday?
B: No, I ________. Only if we're really busy.

3 A: Do you ________ to call your boss by his surname?
B: No, I ________. I usually call him Alberto.

4 A: I don't really like my boss. ________ I look for a new job?
B: No, you ________. Ask yourself why you don't like him.

5 A: ________ you need to check my presentation?
B: No, I ________. I'm sure it's fine.

6 A: ________ I ask you something?
B: Yes, of course you ________. What do you want to know?

4 Complete this article. Use one word from the box in each gap.

encourages increase ~~casual~~ guidelines challenging employees morale ideas

Google now has offices all over the world, but all of them share the same informal corporate culture and [1] *casual* dress code. One of the company's [2] ________ is 'You can be serious without a suit.' Google wants to make its [3] ________ feel important. To improve employee [4] ________, they receive free on-site medical treatment, three free meals a day and access to free sport facilities. To [5] ________ motivation, Google [6] ________ its engineers to spend 20 per cent of their free time working on their own projects. Some of Google's best [7] ________ come from this time off. Google is a company which wants its staff to be happy and enthusiastic about their work. Another corporate guideline is 'Work should be [8] ________ and the challenge should be fun.'

1 14 Listen to Douglas explaining how to sell something on the internet and put these instructions in the correct order.

a State your shipping fees ☐
b Do some research about what people want and prices ☐
c Set a low opening price ☐
d Find the right category ☐
e Include a good photo and an accurate description ☐

2 Listen again and complete these sentences.

1 First, you ________ do some research.

2 ________ ________, you have to find the right category for your items.

3 ________ ________ it's clear, understandable and contains as much detail as possible.

4 ________ ________. And try not to hide any problems because people will probably complain when they get the item.

5 ________, you ________ set a low opening price.

6 Finally, ________ ________ to state your shipping fees but don't make them too high.

3 Complete these sentences. Use one word from the box in each gap.

zoom in delete password print click save paste select

1 You've made the changes, now don't forget to ________ them.

2 Don't choose a ________ that's easy to guess.

3 Try not to ________ the mouse button too fast.

4 You can ________ to make the text bigger and easier to read.

5 First, copy the picture and then ________ it into a new document.

6 To create a new file, first right click the mouse and then ________ 'create new file'.

7 You can ________ old files that you don't need.

8 You shouldn't ________ all your emails – it's bad for the environment.

4 15 Listen to some people giving instructions and decide which are helpful (H) and which are unhelpful (U).

1 ☐

2 ☐

3 ☐

5 Listen again and complete the instructions.

1

1 ________ ________ to mix them up.

2 You ________ ________ wash out the plastic containers first.

3 ________, there's the green bin.

4 OK. Is ________ ________?

2

1 ________ your application in a new document.

2 ________ your photo.

3 ________ ________ to put your present job first.

4 No. ________ ________ back to the top. Delete your date of birth.

3

1 Right. ________, insert the battery into the battery charger.

2 ________. ________. Then you need to plug the battery charger into the power outlet.

3 ________ ________. It takes about two hours.

4 ________ ________ to remove the battery when it's charged.

1 Match idioms 1–6 with the correct meanings a–f.

1 throw in the towel
2 time out
3 give it your best shot
4 get off the hook
5 create a level playing field
6 call the shots

a to take a break
b to create an equal chance for everyone
c to give up
d to be in charge/make the rules
e to avoid responsibility for something/take no responsibility
f to try your hardest

2 Complete these sentences. Use one idiom from exercise 1 in each gap.

1 A lot of candidates applied for the job. We need to ________ and give everyone a fair interview.

2 It's too early to give up. You shouldn't ________ because you think you have no chance.

3 You're working under great pressure. You need to take some ________ and relax.

4 I know you think you have very little chance of getting the job because the other candidates have more experience but you should ________ at the interview and show them what you can do.

5 Although Jones is the manager of the company, it's really Davies who ________. He makes all the important decisions.

6 You made the mistake so don't try to ________ by saying you didn't have enough information.

3 Complete this article. Choose the correct words and expressions.

GEOCACHE – GLOBAL TREASURE HUNTING

Geocaching is a worldwide game of hiding and seeking treasure that [1] (*can*) / *should* be played by anyone. Players place treasure or caches somewhere in the world, find its location using navigation technology and then [2] *have to / shouldn't* share its existence and location on the internet. You [3] *need to / don't have to* have navigation technology to play the game. It might sound easy, but you [4] *shouldn't / can't* always get directly to a cache. Time management and strategic thinking are necessary. Players [5] *have to / mustn't* find the best route. There might be a river in the way, or the cache might be located on the side of a mountain or cliff. The cache [6] *can / should* also be placed underwater so you might [7] *needn't / need to* be able to scuba dive. Before setting out on a search you [8] *must / mustn't* calculate the risks involved.

4 Match these sentence halves to make rules for geocaching.

GEOCACHE RULES

1 You should respect the environment
2 You shouldn't put anything dangerous or illegal in a cache
3 Write about your find in the cache diary
4 You shouldn't put food items in a cache
5 If you take something from a cache,

a then replace it with something else of similar value.
b and then share your experience online with the geocaching community.
c so always take your trash home with you.
d as this is against the law and children also hide and seek caches.
e because animals could find your cache and eat it!

8

A Present perfect
B *yet* and *already*
C **Communication strategies** Sharing ideas
D **Interaction** Dealing with change

What's the big idea?

A Present perfect

1 16 Listen to two people talking about a mobile phone and decide if the statements are true (T) or false (F).

1 Kate's grandmother doesn't use the mobile phone that Kate gave her because it's too complicated. ☐

2 Kate has thought about buying a mobile phone designed for older people. ☐

3 The mobile phone John's mother uses has five speed-dial buttons. ☐

4 The speed-dial button can ring up to five emergency numbers. ☐

5 John's mother hasn't had any trouble using the phone. ☐

6 John's mother had to read the manual before she could use the phone. ☐

2 Listen again and complete these sentences.

1 Yes, well, older people sometimes have problems using modern technology because the designers ________ ________ too many features.

2 ________ you ________ about buying her a mobile phone designed specially for older people?

3 No, I ________ ________ anyone made phones like that.

4 ________ your mother ________ any trouble using it?

5 ________ been ________ it for about a month …

6 … and she says she ________ even ________ the manual.

3 Complete these sentences. Use the verbs in the box and the present perfect.

not work forget ~~update~~ change not read have make decide

1 I *'ve updated* the software and now everything's working again.

2 I ________ the manual so I don't know how that function works.

3 ________ you ________ a note of your username and password?

4 My company ________ recently ________ to let us all work from home two days a week.

5 I can't get any money out of the machine because I ________ my PIN number again.

6 Sally ________ six jobs and she's only 30!

7 ________ Fred ________ his mobile phone provider again? I can't reach him on this number.

8 He ________ with this software before, but I don't think he will have any trouble using it.

4 Complete these conversations. Write the questions.

1 A: *Have you tried calling the hotline* ?
B: No, I haven't tried calling the hotline. I think I can repair it.

2 A: ________________________________?
B: Yes, I've ordered some more paper. It'll be delivered this afternoon.

3 A: ________________________________?
B: No, we haven't updated the files. We'll do it next week.

4 A: ________________________________?
B: Yes, Sarah's sent you the parts you need. Haven't they arrived?

5 A: ________________________________?
B: No, the service engineer hasn't finished repairing the photocopier. Why don't you use the one on the second floor?

6 A: ________________________________?
B: Yes, they've sent the manual, but I haven't had time to read it.

3 yet and already

1 Read about some of the things *The Ladies Home Journal* of December 1900 thought would happen by the 21st century. Which of the things it predicted have already happened and which ones haven't happened yet?

		Has already happened	Hasn't happened yet
1	It will be possible to travel from America to England in less than three days.	✓	
2	The population of the USA will probably be about 350,000,000 to 500,000,000.		
3	The average American will live to be 50 – and not 35 as in 1900.		
4	Express trains will travel at 150 miles per hour.		
5	Cars and houses will be automatically cooled.		
6	Colour photography will be possible.		
7	There will be no mosquitoes or flies.		
8	You will be able to buy ready-cooked meals from shops like our bakeries of today.		

(Adapted from 'What May Happen in the Next Hundred Years', *The Ladies Home Journal*,® December 1900 (written by John Elfreth Watkins, Jr.). Used with permission from Meredith Corporation. All Rights Reserved.)

2 Complete these sentences with *already* or *yet*.

1 Have you *already* sent the report to headquarters?

2 I haven't had time to finish the product presentation ________.

3 I'm afraid I've ________ paid for the flight, so we can't change our plans now.

4 We haven't had any problems with the new computers ________.

5 There's an email here saying they have ________ sent the digital camera you ordered.

6 We haven't decided which system to buy ________.

7 Have you spoken to Mike about the idea ________?

8 We've ________ tested the product in the lab, but we haven't tested it in the field ________.

3 Complete these conversations. Write the questions. Use the words in brackets.

1 A: *Have you read the user manual already*?
(the user manual/already)
B: No, I haven't read it yet.

2 A: ________________________________?
(your new camera/yet)
B: Yes, I've taken about 200 photos with it already!

3 A: ________________________________?
(the navigation system/yet)
B: Yes, I've used the navigation system and it works very well.

4 A: ________________________________?
(that function/yet)
B: No, I haven't used it yet because I don't know what it's for.

5 A: ________________________________?
(the meeting/already)
B: No, it hasn't finished yet.

6 A: ________________________________?
(the new software/already)
B: No, I haven't installed it yet; I'll do it at the weekend.

4 Look at Henry's list of things to do. Write about what he has already done and what he has not done yet. Use the present perfect and *already* or *yet*.

1 *He's already changed the £500 to euros.*
2 ________________________________
3 ________________________________
4 ________________________________
5 ________________________________
6 ________________________________
7 ________________________________
8 ________________________________

1 Look at these problems. Then use the prompts in brackets to make recommendations, proposals or suggestions.

1 I feel so tired when I get up in the morning.

I suggest going to bed earlier. (suggest/go to bed earlier)

2 The traffic is terrible in this area and there's nowhere to park. ______________________. (recommend/come/by train)

3 What do you think we should do with the money they gave us? ______________________? (Why don't/give it/charity)

4 Where shall we open the European office?

______________________? (How about/open it/Krakow)

5 What's the best way to get from the airport to your office? ______________________. (suggest/take/a taxi)

6 How can we get more people to buy this product?

______________________. (could/reduce the price)

2 Match suggestions 1–6 with responses a–f.

1 Why don't you look for a house that's nearer to your company?

2 How about going to Egypt for a holiday?

3 What about going to work by bicycle?

4 How about throwing some of these old magazines away?

5 Why don't we have the party on Thursday evening?

6 Why don't you buy a second-hand laptop on eBay?

a I'll look into it, but I think it's a bit too hot there in August.

b No, there are some interesting articles in them.

c Yes, but don't forget most of us have to work the next day.

d Yes, but I like living in the countryside.

e I don't think that's a very good idea. It might break down.

f Yes, that would be a good idea in the summer but what about in the winter?

3 Read this article about a well-designed office and how it can help staff to be more productive. Then decide whether the statements are true (T) or false (F).

According to surveys, companies could be losing billions of dollars because of badly designed workplaces. So what does a well-designed office look like?

Most of us probably think of offices that let in lots of light, are full of expensive furniture and plants. That is important, but other factors may be more important.

Architects recommend designing workspaces that do not just have areas for when we are working alone and concentrating on specific tasks but that we design workplaces where there are areas for teamwork and exchanging ideas and knowledge.

Finally, they suggest designing special areas where employees can socialize and talk about non-work topics such as what they did at the weekend or what they are planning to do for their next holiday.

If there is enough space for these areas employees will be more motivated and productive. And you don't need to build a new office building; very often these spaces can be created by redesigning old offices.

1 A survey suggests that companies could save billions of dollars by redesigning workplaces. ☐

2 Having a bright office, full of expensive furniture and plants is the most important factor. ☐

3 Architects recommend having areas for teamwork, learning, socializing and where you can work on your own. ☐

4 Companies also need to have areas so that employees can read books and watch TV. ☐

5 Companies that don't provide these spaces will be less productive. ☐

6 These spaces can be provided in existing office buildings ☐

1 Match phrases 1–6 with collocations a–f.

1 think about an idea
2 think of an idea
3 a great idea
4 a new idea
5 a crazy idea
6 reject an idea

a dismiss an idea
b an original idea
c a ridiculous idea
d a brilliant idea
e come up with an idea
f consider an idea

2 Complete these sentences. Use a collocation with *idea* from exercise 1 in each gap.

1 Jane has had *a great idea*! I think it could save the company millions.

2 Serving tea and coffee on the airport train is ________. The train's always full and the passengers put their luggage in the aisle.

3 That's ________. I wonder why nobody has thought about doing that before.

4 I'm afraid we have to ________ even if it is a good one, if it costs more than it saves.

5 We always ________ carefully before we invest in it.

6 Could you help me ________ for a new slogan? I can't think of anything.

3 Match slogans a–d with the correct products 1–4.

1 *Digital camera*

2 *Washing-up liquid*

3 *Bar of chocolate*

4 *Toothpaste*

a ***Sparkling dishes in half the time!***
b ***Every bite as delicious as the last.***
c ***Minty fresh!***
d ***Perfect photos with just one click.***

4 Read this article and choose the best title a–d.

a **Global advertising**
b **Making contacts in business**
c **Marketing on a small budget**
d **How to sell more coffee**

Marketing and advertising campaigns can cost millions but there are lots of ways small businesses can find new customers without spending a fortune. Here are just three.

1
Freebies and giveaways are an excellent way of marketing for a new company. A new coffee shop could, for example, offer a free doughnut to the first 500 customers. If the customers think it was a good deal, they will come back and may bring their friends. Giveaways help your customer remember you over the competition.

2
Loyalty programmes are a good way of building up sales with existing customers. Examples of this are giving customers points for buying things from you and offering something free or much cheaper when the customer has earned enough points. People will come back if they think they are earning something for 'free'.

3
Competitions are also a great way to attract customers because people love winning prizes. Be creative and try to make the competition fun; you may even attract the local press and get some free advertising. Competitions are also a good way of building up a mailing list which you can use later to advertise new products or special offers.

5 Look at the article again and match marketing techniques 1–3 with benefits a–c.

1 giveaways
2 loyalty programmes
3 competitions

a help to build up a mailing list of customers
b help customers to remember you
c encourage customers to come back

9

A Modals of possibility
B Future arrangements
C **Communication strategies** Saying 'no'
D **Interaction** Planning a social event

Put it in your diary

A Modals of possibility

1 Complete this article. Choose the correct form in *italics*.

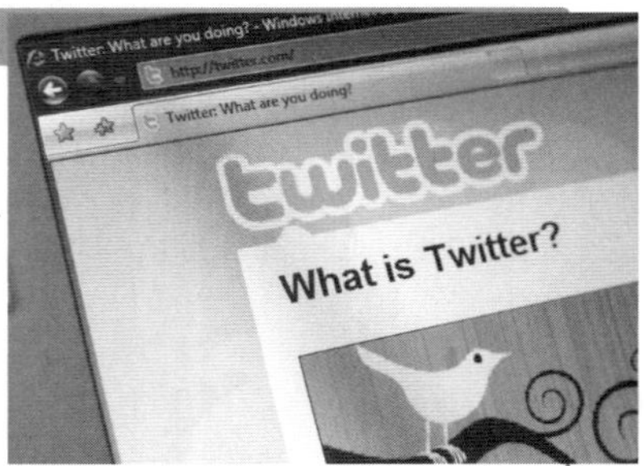

Twitter is a website where people can communicate using instant messaging. The instant messages – also known as tweets – are about users' daily lives. It now has more than 30 million users all over the world. Experts predict this number 1 *will / won't* double in the next few years. 2 *Couldn't / Could* they be right?

It is a great service for busy people who 3 *may not / won't* have time to keep in touch with large numbers of people. Twitter can also post instant news about important events, like earthquakes and plane crashes, as they are happening and this use 4 *will / may not* grow in importance.

Companies now know how they can use Twitter to inform customers and spread information about products. This 5 *might / couldn't* be a new way of marketing in the future.

2 Find words and phrases in the article which mean the same as the following.

1 to say what will happen in the future ________
2 to increase twice as much ________
3 to have a lot to do ________
4 to stay connected with other people ________
5 things that happen ________
6 to pass around or distribute ________

3 Complete these conversations. Put the words in brackets in the correct order to make questions.

1 A: Could I speak to Matt Reynolds, please?
B: I'm afraid he's not in the office. Could I help you instead? (help/ instead/I/ you/Could)

2 A: I can't complete the report without help.
B: ____________________? (John/know/Might/some/the/information/of)

3 A: We need to send out this list of invitations today.
B: ____________________? (have/I/look/May/a/list/the/at)

4 A: We won't complete the project on time.
B: ____________________? (us/help/Will/you)

5 A: We have a lot to discuss …
B: Excuse me. ____________________? (question/quick/I/a/Might/ask)

6 A: The report for Mexico is urgent.
B: ____________________? (later/this/you/Could/stay/evening)

4 Complete these sentences. Choose the correct answers.

1 Harry has already left the office so he ________ know about the meeting we planned this afternoon.
a will
b (mightn't)
c may

2 The party starts at eight. ________ you come a bit earlier to help me prepare the food?
a Could
b May
c Might

3 Molly is such a fantastic accountant. I'm sure she ________ get the job.
a could
b will
c might

4 The company wasn't happy with our work so we ________ get the contract next time.
a may not
b will
c couldn't

5 Half the team is on holiday or sick. We ________ finish the project on time.
a may
b won't
c could

6 I'm a bit busy at the moment! ________ I call you back later?
a Mightn't
b Could
c Will

1 Complete these sentences about future arrangements. Use a verb from the box in the present continuous.

arrive attend schedule invite meet ~~build~~

1 The company _is building_ the new factory in Bulgaria to save costs.

2 I _______ the appointment for 2 p.m. to give you time to get here from the airport.

3 We _______ around one hundred guests so we need to book a large room.

4 You _______ a meeting at 8 a.m. so don't forget your presentation.

5 I _______ my virtual assistant in Mumbai for the first time next Monday although he started to work for me two years ago.

6 He _______ at the airport at 2 a.m. so I'll pick him up and take him to his hotel.

2 Complete these conversations. Use a question word from the box and the verbs in brackets in the present continuous.

who ~~what~~ why where how long how

1 A: _What time are you arriving at the airport_? (arrive)
B: We're arriving at the airport at 4 p.m.

2 A: ________________________________? (get)
B: We're taking a taxi from the airport to the hotel.

3 A: ________________________________? (stay)
B: We're staying at the Hilton.

4 A: ________________________________? (meet)
B: We're meeting Ms Allwood.

5 A: ________________________________? (meet)
B: We're meeting her because she's the head of finance and she can answer all our questions.

6 A: ________________________________? (stay)
B: We're staying for three days.

3 Rewrite these sentences. Use the words in brackets and the present continuous.

1 We meet our London colleagues every two weeks.
We're meeting our London colleagues next Monday
(meet/London colleagues/next Monday)

2 Alan usually goes on business trips five times a year.
________________ (go on/a business trip/in April)

3 Ryan never goes to parties.
________________ (not go/the party/next Saturday)

4 Does Claire organize conferences?
________________ (Claire/organize/the next conference?)

5 Patrick never flies to meetings.
________________ (not fly/the meeting in March)

6 Do you travel to India regularly?
________________ (you/travel/India/next week?)

4 17 Listen to this conversation and complete the notes about the changes to Laura's schedule.

5 Listen again and complete these sentences.

a It's going great, thanks. I 1 _______ back on Saturday morning.

b Your first appointment at 8:00 is cancelled. You 2 _______ a telephone conference with Frank in New York instead.

c John wants to speak to you 3 _______ so you 4 _______ him for a working lunch at 12:00.

d The 2:00 meeting is still on, but you 5 _______ to Mike's office as he has 6 _______ all day.

e At 3:00 you 7 _______ to the airport for your 8 _______ with Tony Lee as planned.

C Communication strategies Saying 'no'

1 Decide if these expressions are Preparing to invite (P), Inviting (I), Accepting (A), Saying No (N) or Responding to No (R).

1. I'd be delighted to come. What time should I be there? (A)
2. Are you doing anything on Saturday evening? ( )
3. OK. Not to worry. ( )
4. I'd love to come but I'm doing something else on Saturday. ( )
5. Would you like to come to the cinema? ( )
6. Thanks. I'd love to be there. ( )
7. Thanks for asking but I'm afraid I'm busy at the weekend. ( )
8. Sorry I can't make it. ( )
9. Do you have any plans for tomorrow? ( )
10. I can't wait to come! ( )
11. Oh, that's a shame. ( )
12. Thanks for the invitation. Can I bring a friend, too? ( )

2 Put these conversations in the correct order.

1

a Sure. That sounds great. I love his films. ( )

b Are you doing anything on Sunday afternoon? ( )

c Sure. See you then. ( )

d Why? What's going on? ( )

e OK. See you around 3 p.m.? ( )

f There's a new Jason Deep film showing at the cinema. Do you want to come and see it? ( )

2

a Not to worry. ( )

b Have you got any plans for Saturday evening? ( )

c I don't think so … Why? ( )

d Oh. That sounds lovely … but actually I've just remembered Jane and I already have plans to see my brother and his wife on Saturday. Sorry. ( )

e We're having a party to celebrate Jack's retirement. Would you like to come? ( )

3 Match these sentences with the correct responses.

1. I'm afraid we can't come.
2. Are you doing anything this weekend?
3. Would you like to join us for dinner?
4. Maybe another time.
5. Thanks for the invitation. Can I let you know?

a Yes, we'd love to.

b Oh, that's a shame.

c Why? What's going on?

d Yes, but not later than Thursday.

e OK. How about next Sunday?

4 18 Listen to three conversations. Decide who accepts (A), who hesitates (H) and who refuses (R) each invitation.

Conversation 1 ( )

Conversation 2 ( )

Conversation 3 ( )

5 Listen again and complete the sentences.

1 A: Are you [1] _doing_ _anything_ _special_ on Saturday?
B: Not [2] ______. Why?
A: Well, we're having some people round. [3] ______ ______ ______ to come?
B: Sounds [4] ______. Can I check the time and [5] ______ ______ to you?
A: Can you [6] ______ ______ ______ by Friday?

2 A: Have you [7] ______ ______ ______ for Saturday?
B: Why? What's [8] ______ ______?
A: We're [9] ______ a small get-together at my house. Can you [10] ______ ______?
B: It's nice of you to think of me. I'd [11] ______ ______ ______. Thanks.

3 A: [12] ______ ______ ______ to join us for coffee on Sunday afternoon?
B: Oh, I'm [13] ______ I'm completely booked up the whole weekend.
A: [14] ______ ______. Maybe another time.

1 Complete these sentences. Use the correct form of *give* and a word from the box.

advice	~~message~~	talk	smile	reason	time

1 Could you __*give*__ John a __*message*__, please? Tell him I can't make the 2 p.m. appointment.
2 I haven't finished the report yet. Could you _______ me more _______? I think I need two more days.
3 I _______ a _______ on 'Riding in Argentina' last Saturday. About 50 people came.
4 OK. Everybody _______ me a big _______ so I can take a good photo. Say cheese!
5 It's OK to turn down the invitation but I think you should _______ a _______ and explain why you can't go.
6 We've been invited to the Queen's garden party. Can you _______ me some _______ about what to wear and how to behave?

2 Match the different types of party a–f to the correct photos.

a Halloween party
b fancy dress party
c dinner party
d birthday party
e retirement party
f house warming party

1 ☐

2 ☐

3 ☐

4 ☐

5 ☐

6 ☐

3 Complete these sentences. Use one type of party from exercise 2 in each gap.

1 I'm going to be 21 next Saturday. Would you like to come to my __*birthday party*__?
2 Our new house is finished and we moved in last week. We'd love you to come to our _____________.
3 Are you planning to dress up as a ghost or a monster for Janet's _____________?
4 I'm glad you can come to our _____________ on Friday. Do you eat fish?
5 Can I borrow your cowboy costume for the _____________?
6 All Ali's colleagues are going to his _____________. They're going to give him a watch.

4 Complete this email. Use one word from the box in each gap.

attending	apologize	schedule	invitation	diary	may	get-together

Hi Jo,

Thanks for the 1 _______ to your birthday party. I can't give you a definite yes. I've just checked my 2 _______ and I see that I'm 3 _______ a conference on that Saturday and there's going to be a 4 _______ for our suppliers afterwards. If everything is on 5 _______ and I leave at 7 p.m. I 6 _______ only be one hour late. It's Saturday, though and the traffic might be heavy so if I'm really late, or I don't make it, I 7 _______ now.

Cheers,
Belinda

5 Complete the puzzle and find the hidden word.

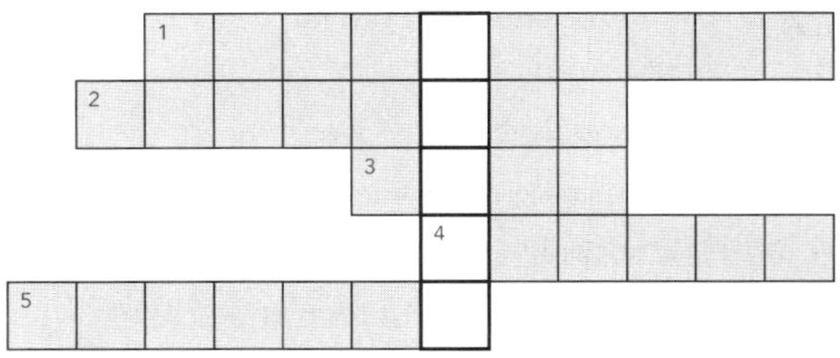

Clues:
1 Another word for *arranging* times
2 If you don't know your friends have arranged a party, then it is a …
3 If you're not on time, you're …
4 The opposite of *accept* an invitation
5 An organization that helps people, for example by giving food to homeless people

10

A Countable and uncountable nouns
B *too* and *enough*
C **Communication strategies** Complaints
D **Interaction** Collecting information

Special places

A Countable and uncountable nouns

1 19 Listen to a conversation between Bob Thomas, an estate agent and Pat Kennedy, a business woman looking for new offices and complete Pat's notes.

1 *How much office space is for rent? _________ M2*
2 *How many cars can park in the underground car park? Approx _________*
3 *How much does a parking space cost per car per month? £ _________*
4 *How much is the rent for the office space and parking per month? £ _________*

2 Decide whether these nouns are countable (C) or uncountable (U).

1	time	*U*	7	people	☐
2	space	☐	8	office	☐
3	shop	☐	9	money	☐
4	railway station	☐	10	workplace	☐
5	restaurant	☐	11	square feet	☐
6	rent	☐	12	electricity	☐

3 Here are some things you could ask about a new office. Complete the questions with *How much* or *How many*.

1 *How many* lifts are there in the building?
2 ____________ square metres can we rent on this floor?
3 ____________ does a square metre cost to rent?
4 ____________ offices are there on this floor?
5 ____________ space is for rent?
6 ____________ people could work in this office?
7 ____________ companies are there in this building?
8 ____________ time do we have to make a decision?

4 Complete these sentences. Choose the correct answers.

1 *There is a lot of / There are a lot of* empty office buildings in the city centre.

2 *There isn't much / There aren't much* time to find somewhere to move to.

3 *There isn't any / There aren't any* good restaurants in the area.

4 *Is there a lot / Are there a lot* of space in your office?

5 *Is there much / Are there many* parking spaces in the street?

6 *There isn't any / There aren't* any air-conditioning in the building.

5 Complete these tips to help senior citizens find the right place to move to. Use the words in brackets.

- Don't move somewhere where [1] *there isn't any* public transport. **(any)**
- [2] ____________ shops near the house or flat? **(many)**
- Avoid houses or flats where [3] ____________ stairs to climb. **(a lot of)**
- [4] ____________ people in the area who can help if you need it? Having friends or relatives to help is always good. **(any)**
- If you don't have any friends or relatives in the area, [5] ____________ community services available? **(any)**
- Try to stay active; try to find a community where [6] ____________ activities and events for senior citizens. **(a lot of)**

B too and enough

1 20 Listen to some complaints from guests staying at two different hotels. Decide if the statements are true (T) or false (F).

Conversation 1

1 The 20-minute walk to the beach from the hotel is too dangerous. ☐

2 The cliff path from the hotel to the beach is too dangerous to use. ☐

3 The guest says the building work in the new hotel is too noisy. ☐

Conversation 2

4 The guest wants to change rooms because the view isn't nice enough. ☐

5 The guest's room gets too hot during the day and too cold at night. ☐

6 The Nelson suite isn't cheap enough. ☐

2 Complete these sentences. Then listen again and check.

Conversation 1

a I'm afraid I'm [1] ________ ________ happy with the hotel we're in. It's [2] ________ ________ from the beach and another hotel is being built next to it …

b Yes, but now it's a 20-minute walk from the hotel to the beach because we can't use the cliff path. It's [3] ________ ________.

c … and it's *bang, bang, bang, bang* until ten o'clock at night. It's [4] ________.

Conversation 2

d … it's a lovely view but the room gets [5] ________ ________ during the day and it doesn't [6] ________ ________ ________ at night, even with the air-conditioning on.

e $120! Oh, no, that's [7] ________ ________.

f That's fine. A twin room's [8] ________ ________. We'll take that.

3 Complete these sentences. Use a phrase from the box in each gap.

is too	are too	is too much	are too many

1 £7,500 *is too much* for a one-week safari tour.

2 I don't want to go there for a holiday. There ____________ tourists there in the summer.

3 It's a nice restaurant, but I'm afraid it ____________ expensive.

4 They can't be the real thing; they ____________ cheap to be original.

5 It would be great if we could see all those places, but it ____________ far to drive in a week.

6 I wouldn't want to go camping in a jungle, there ________ insects and snakes there.

4 Complete these sentences. Add *enough* in the correct place in each sentence.

1 I don't think we'll have ^*enough* time to visit the museum today.

2 The hotel isn't really central.

3 Do we have money to buy the tickets or do I need to change some?

4 It's 80 km around the lake and that's long for my first bike ride this year.

5 Do you think the weather will be warm to go camping there in March?

6 We wanted to go skiing, but there wasn't snow.

5 Complete these sentences. Put the words in brackets in the correct order.

1 *These jeans are too expensive* (too/jeans/These/expensive/are). I'm not going to buy them.

2 ____________________________ (enough/I/don't have/money). Can you lend me some?

3 ____________________________ (hot/is/very/in here/It/)! I'll open the window.

4 I'm going to complain. ____________________________ (this morning/hot water/for a shower/enough/There wasn't).

5 ____________________________ (people/There/too/in the pool/were/many) so I went to the beach.

6 ____________________________ (space/There/on the bus/enough/wasn't) so we had to wait for another one.

C Communication strategies | Complaints

1 Read this article and decide whether the statements are true (T) or false (F).

Praising and complaining

We usually complain about what we don't like, but have you ever thought about writing to a company to thank them for doing a good job?

You expect a company to do a good job, so why should you write to them to tell them they are doing something properly?

Everybody likes praise; it helps us to keep up the good work. Without it we might not make that extra effort – why should we if nobody thanks us for it?

Companies often send out questionnaires and surveys to ask their customers what they think of a product. This information may be important, but these statistics are never worth as much as a personal letter or phone call thanking the company or the individuals behind the product or service.

Complaining can be useful because it helps a company to make a product or service better but praising is just as useful because it motivates the staff and helps the company to understand what it is doing well.

1 The author thinks we are more likely to complain than to praise. ☐

2 Most of us don't praise because we expect a good service or product. ☐

3 Nobody really appreciates praise so why bother? ☐

4 One way of finding out what customers think about a product is to ask them to complete a questionnaire or survey. ☐

5 The information in the questionnaires and surveys isn't really important. ☐

6 The author thinks that praising is more important than complaining. ☐

2 Choose the best responses to these complaints.

1 Every time I try to open the program my PC crashes.

a I'm very sorry about that. Would you like to buy a new one?

b That's very frustrating for you. Bring your PC in and we'll take a look at it.

c It must be your hardware that's causing the problem.

2 I bought this GPS last week but it doesn't work.

a Oh dear. Well, we'd be happy to replace it.

b That's annoying. Didn't you read the instruction manual properly?

c I'm sorry about that. That's bad luck.

3 It stopped working three weeks after the guarantee ran out.

a Yes, that's normal.

b We'll replace it for free but we'll have to charge you for the labour. Is that OK?

c You should have paid a bit more to extend the guarantee.

4 The bill you sent us was for parts that we didn't order.

a I don't believe that. Someone must have ordered them.

b That's a pity but these things happen.

c Yes, I'm very sorry about that. We mixed up your order with another customer's

5 You sent me three copies of this book. I only ordered one.

a Oh, I'm really sorry about that. I'll check our customer data base to see what happened. It won't happen again.

b Really? Why didn't you send the ones you didn't need back to us?

c What do you want me to do about it?

6 I don't know why you can't find my reservation. Here's an email from you confirming a single room for three nights.

a Well, you're not in the computer so I'm afraid there's nothing I can do about it.

b Yes, well if you come back on Wednesday, we may have a room for you.

c I'm very sorry about that. I can offer you a double room at the same price.

1 Read this travel article about three cities. Then match each city A–C with the correct paragraph 1–3.

A Brasilia, Brazil

B Chicago, USA

C Damascus, Syria

☐ 1
This city was planned and developed in 1956 and is listed as a World Heritage Site by UNESCO. Some people love its large avenues and the modern architecture, but other people hate it. The city's artificial* lake has an 80 km shoreline*. It attracts a lot of wake boarders and windsurfers.

☐ 2
This city has a population of about 4,000,000 and is one of the oldest cities in the world. It is famous for its mosques, covered markets, palaces and its cafés and excellent restaurants. The mountains, 50 km to the northwest, attract skiers in the winter. The city's transport consists of minibuses. There is no underground train system.

☐ 3
With a population of 2.8 million this is the fourth largest city in the country. It is located on the shore of a 58,000 km^2 lake and although it is not well known for its sandy beaches and water sports this is a great place to do them. The city is home to many famous museums and art galleries, but most people think of the city's skyscrapers when they hear its name.

artificial = not made of natural things but made to be like something that is real or natural

shoreline = the land along the edge of a large area of water

2 Look at the article again and answer these questions.

1 Is Brasilia an ancient city?
2 Is Brasilia a good place to visit if you like water sports?
3 Is Damascus an interesting place to visit if you like culture and history?
4 Does it snow in the mountains near Damascus?
5 Is Chicago the biggest city in the USA?
6 Is Chicago a good place to visit if you like lying on the beach?

3 Read sentences 1–6 giving tourist information and advice. Then match each sentence with the correct category a–f.

1 The gardens are open to the public and the best time to visit them is in the late spring or early summer. ☐

2 It takes ages to get to the airport by bus; it's best to take the train but it can be expensive. ☐

3 I'd highly recommend visiting the market in the fourth district. ☐

4 You'll need a week if you want to visit all the major museums and art galleries in the city. ☐

5 The castle was built by King Ludwig II in the nineteenth century. ☐

6 The old town is full of bars, discos and small theatres. ☐

a historical buildings
b culture
c nightlife
d parks and gardens
e public transport
f shopping

11

A First conditional
B *if* and *when*
C **Communication strategies** Agree or disagree
D **Interaction** Introducing changes

Making changes

A First conditional

1 **Match sentence halves 1–8 with a–h.**

1 If we give the company a discount
2 Mike will probably leave the company
3 If you work 12 hours a day, every day
4 If I have a problem with the computer
5 If I don't finish these reports
6 If I lose my job
7 We will fire employees
8 I'll buy a new car

a you'll get ill and collapse.
b I'll have to work late this evening.
c if we catch them stealing.
d they may place their next order with us.
e if I get a pay rise.
f if we don't give him a pay rise.
g I'll ask Steffi in IT to help me.
h I'll go to Australia and get a job there.

2 **Complete these sentences. Use *worth* and the words in brackets.**

1 This television is so old: it's *not worth repairing* (not/repair). Let's buy a new one.

2 If you want to get a good pension when you retire, it's ________ (pay) into a pension fund when you're young.

3 Look at that diamond necklace it ________ (be) $250, 000! I can't afford it.

4 The new exhibition is really ________ (see). I enjoyed it very much.

5 If I study for an MBA I might get a better job. But ________ (be/it) it?

6 Don't throw out these old comics! They might ________ (be) a lot of money.

7 The company is making losses at the moment. Is it ________ (ask) my boss for a pay rise?

8 It's ________ (not/work) overtime. You should go home and relax instead.

3 **Complete this interview. Put the verbs in brackets in the first conditional.**

Jeff: We're doing an article on generation Y – people born between 1977 and 2002 – and their attitudes to work. You're a member of this generation; can I ask you a few questions?

Arni: Sure.

Jeff: First of all, how old are you and how do you view work?

Arni: I'm 27 and I work to live, not live to work – like my Dad. If he [1] *works* (work) any harder, he *'ll collapse* (collapse)! He [2] ________ (feel) bad if he ________ (go) home after ten hours in the office. If he [3] ________ (take) time off work he ________ (not relax). I don't think it's worth it. I don't want to change my job too often but if my job [4] ________ (not be) interesting, I ________ (look) for another opportunity.

Jeff: But what about your career? If you [5] ________ (change) jobs too often you ________ (not get) to the top.

Arni: [6] ________ (you, be) happy if you ________ (get) to the top? Probably not …

Jeff: An interesting point. Thanks for talking to me today …

1 Complete these sentences with *if* or *when*.

1 __*When*__ I come home this evening we can have dinner together. I'll be there at seven o'clock.

2 ________ I wake up in the morning, I always switch on the radio to get the news.

3 ________ I hear Sue tell the same joke again, I'll go crazy.

4 We won't get tickets for the show ________ we don't book them today.

5 ________ you think your staff are stealing, you should install video cameras.

6 I'll probably go travelling in Asia for six months ________ I retire.

7 ________ we don't recruit more top people, we won't be competitive.

8 You'll hear from us ________ we look at your application next week.

2 Match sentence halves 1–8 with a–h. Then write *if* or *when* to complete the sentences.

1 You can get any job you want **c**

2 John can help me with the drinks

3 You get a gold watch from the company

4 Just ask for a translation

5 You're going to miss your flight

6 I want to buy shares

7 What are you going to do

8 I always take my mobile with me

a ________ you lose your job?

b ________ you don't leave now.

c __*if*__ you have the right qualifications.

d ________ you don't understand the text.

e ________ I go on holiday. I need to be available all the time.

f ________ you retire.

g ________ the stock market opens tomorrow morning.

h ________ he arrives early.

3 Complete these sentences. Put the verb in brackets in the correct form.

1 We __*'ll ask*__ (ask) for directions if we can't find the restaurant.

2 We ________ (not start) the party until the guests arrive.

3 We had a great time when we ________ (go) to Argentina.

4 If we work as a team we ________ (be) more productive.

5 If we ________ (not leave) a big tip the waiter might be angry.

6 This TV is very old. If it breaks down again we ________ (not repair) it.

7 We ________ (not sign) the contract unless we reach an agreement.

8 I _____ (wait) outside the train station when you arrive.

4 Match the beginnings and endings of these sentences to make quotes or sayings.

1 An ounce of action **c**

2 When the well's dry,

3 Nothing in the world is worth having

4 A picture

5 If something is worth doing,

6 Only a life lived for others

a we know the worth of water. *(Benjamin Franklin)*

b is worth a thousand words.

c is worth a ton of theory. *(Friedrich Engels)*

d is a life worthwhile. *(Albert Einstein)*

e if it comes too easy.

f it's worth doing well.

Benjamin Franklin

Friedrich Engels

Albert Einstein

1 Complete this article. Use one word from the box in each gap.

public	secret	permission	re-install	habits	chain	branches	theft

When the supermarket [1] ________ Lidl was caught spying on its workers, top bosses from the firm said they were as surprised as everyone else. Detectives installed tiny, [2] ________ video cameras in the shops. The detectives collected information on employees' work [3] ________, their private lives and their lunch and bathroom breaks.

The scale of the spying in stores throughout Germany and the Czech Republic shocked the [4] ________. It was a major news story for several weeks.

So will Lidl give up filming altogether? The company said that with 3,000 [5] ________ all over the region that wouldn't work. The cameras are necessary. The company will [6] ________ the cameras in the supermarkets – for the protection of the employees and to guard against [7] ________. But this time, the company will tell employees and ask them to give their [8] ________. The employees will also be able to watch the films at any time.

2 Look at the article again and decide if these statements are true (T) or false (F).

1 The company Lidl was spying on its customers. ☐
2 The top bosses knew about the spying. ☐
3 The detectives only collected information on how the employees did their work. ☐
4 Not many people were interested in the story. ☐
5 Lidl won't install the cameras again. ☐
6 The employees will know about any new cameras. ☐

3 21 Complete these conversations. Use one word or phrase from the box in each gap. Then listen and check.

worth	but they're expensive	security guards	search	staff	could hire	theft	why don't we

1 A: I'm not sure about CCTV cameras in the [1] ________ rest area. Lidl tried it and got very bad publicity.
B: Perhaps it's a better idea to reward staff who report employee [2] ________.

2 A: We [3] ________ a consultant to give us advice on what sort of staff training we need.
B: Training is always [4] ________ it.

3 A: All the stores in London have [5] ________ in uniform at the door. They look tough. I'm sure they stop people even thinking about shoplifting.
B: Yes, [6] ________. Are they really worth it?

4 A: So [7] ________ just hire more sales staff?
B: And we could specially train them to look out for shoplifters and employee theft.

5 A: Maybe we need to [8] ________ our sales staff.
B: Yes, but they'll complain to the union and we'll find ourselves in the newspapers, too.

4 Look at the conversations in exercise 3 and/or listen again. Decide if B is agreeing (A) or disagreeing (D) in each case.

1 (A)
2 ☐
3 ☐
4 ☐
5 ☐

5 Match sentences 1–6 with the correct responses a–f.

1 It's too difficult.
2 Tom is very good at his job.
3 We can't spend any more money.
4 That blue shirt is very nice.
5 He won't agree to that.
6 The schedule is too short.

a Yes, and he's very friendly.
b No, he won't like it.
c Yes, we need more time.
d And it's less expensive than the yellow one.
e Yes, it's very complicated.
f No, we're already over budget.

1 Complete this article. Put the verbs in brackets in the correct form.

What's the best way to keep fit?

Do you do enough exercise to keep fit? Or are you planning to get fit when you retire? If you 1 ________ (not do), then read on …

You 2 ________ (not need) to join a sports club or a gym if you want to get or stay fit. In fact, one of the easiest and cheapest ways to get some exercise is walking. And you can do this at any age. If you walk regularly, it 3 ________ (help) to exercise the muscles in the lower part of your body and walking is good for your heart, too.

Jogging gets you out in the fresh air, but if you 4 ________ (not used to) running, don't start by trying to do a mini-marathon. Try to run for five minutes and add a minute or two to that slowly until you can run for 20 to 30 minutes without stopping.

Cycling is another good way to get fit. Studies show that if you regularly cycle more than 30 km a week you 5 ________ (be) 50 per cent less likely to have a heart attack.

Swimming is ideal if you 6 ________ (have) problems with your bones or joints. A 20-minute swim will exercise nearly all the major muscles in your body.

2 Complete these sentences with *if* or *when*.

1 ________ you don't do any exercise, you'll soon be unfit and overweight.

2 ________ people get older, they tend to do less exercise.

3 ________ your kids go to school, they'll be taught to play a lot of different team sports.

4 ________ you're interested in losing weight, why don't you try this diet?

5 ________ I finish work this evening, I'm going to play squash with Tom.

6 ________ you cycle for an hour, you'll burn about 300 calories.

3 Match verbs 1–6 with nouns/noun phrases a–f to make collocations.

1 give	a your lifestyle
2 install	b money
3 earn	c advice
4 set up	d exercise
5 do	e machines
6 change	f an experiment

4 Complete these sentences. Use one collocation from exercise 3 in the correct form in each gap.

1 We're planning to *install* exercise *machines* in the staff restroom to help employees keep fit.

2 Can I ________ you some ________? Don't resign from your job.

3 We ________ ________ to find out which jobs require the most walking.

4 I'm going to completely ________ my ________ starting today. I want to be fitter and healthier.

5 I'd rather have an interesting job than ________ a lot of ________.

6 You don't look very well. You need to ________ more ________. Start by taking the stairs not the lift every day.

12

A The passive
B Active and passive
C **Communication strategies** Turn taking
D **Interaction** Promoting an event

That's entertainment!

A The passive

1 Read this article about micro-budget films and decide if the statements are true (T) or false (F).

Micro-budget films

What do *The Blair Witch Project* and *Pather Panchali* have in common?

Answer: They were both very successful films and they were both produced for very little money – they are low- or micro-budget films.

There is no official definition of what low-budget films or micro-budget films are but an action film costing US$10 million would probably be called low-budget; a documentary costing US$10 million would not.

Micro-budget films are usually made by young or unknown directors who cannot get money from the big film studios. One example of a successful low-budget film is *The Blair Witch Project*. It was made for US$22,000, but it earned over US$248 million worldwide.

Perhaps the most famous micro-budget films were made by the Bengali film director Satyajit Ray, his most famous being *The Apu Trilogy* (1955–1959). The first film in the trilogy, *Pather Panchali* (1955), was produced on a budget of US$3,000. Many film critics say it is among the greatest films of all time.

1 A micro-budget film is any film costing less than US$10 million to produce. ☐

2 The big film studios often give young or unknown directors a micro budget to make a film. ☐

3 Successful micro-budget films can make a lot of money. ☐

4 *Pather Panchali* is one of three micro-budget films that Satyajit Ray produced between 1955–1959. ☐

5 Many film critics think *Pather Panchali* is one of the best films ever made. ☐

2 Decide if these sentences from the article are passive (P) or active (A).

1 They were all very successful films. (A)

2 They were all produced for very little money. ☐

3 Micro-budget films are usually made by young or unknown directors. ☐

4 The director, Robert Rodriguez, hired mostly amateur actors. ☐

5 The first film in the trilogy was produced on a budget of US$3,000. ☐

6 Many film critics say it is one of the greatest films of all time. ☐

3 Complete these sentences. Put the verbs in brackets into the correct passive form.

1 *Star Wars* _was released_ (release) on 25th May 1977 by 20th Century Fox.

2 The three *Lord of the Rings* movies ________ (film) in New Zealand.

3 *Casablanca* ________ (often describe) as one of the greatest films that has ever been made.

4 The film *The Dark Knight* ________ (base on) the super hero Batman.

5 *Slumdog Millionaire* is a British film about a young man who is one question away from winning 20 million rupees. It ________ (shoot) in Mumbai, India.

6 *Singin' in the Rain* ________ (rank) as the greatest musical film ever made.

4 Match these films with the correct genres.

Film	Genre
1 *Star Wars*	a fantasy
2 *Sleepless in Seattle*	b romance
3 *Austin Powers*	c comedy
4 *Shrek*	d action
5 *Singin' in the Rain*	e sci-fi
6 *The Lord of the Rings*	f musical
7 *Psycho*	g horror
8 *James Bond: Casino Royale*	h animated

B Unsicht-Bar, Berlin, Germany

A Ithaa Underwater Restaurant, Maldives

1 **Look at the photos of two unusual restaurants. Then read the sentences and match them with the correct photos.**

1 It is located five metres below the waves of the Indian Ocean. (A)

2 Guests cannot see anything. The restaurant is completely dark. ☐

3 You can't read the menu in the dining area of the restaurant. ☐

4 Guests are taken to their tables by blind waiters and waitresses. ☐

5 You can watch tropical fish swim past while you are eating your dinner. ☐

6 The walls are made of a special plastic so the diners can see through them. ☐

7 You can be forgiven for drinking out of the wrong glass. ☐

8 The restaurant was built in Singapore and transported to its current location by ship. ☐

2 **Look at the sentences in exercise 1 again. Decide if the sentences are active (A) or passive (P). Which sentence has an active and a passive part to it?**

Active:	Passive:	Both:
☐	(1)	☐
☐	☐	
☐	☐	
☐	☐	

3 **Complete these sentences. Use the verbs in brackets in the correct form: active or passive.**

1 The restaurant isn't very big. It only ________ (seat) about 30 guests.

2 I'm sorry, this table ________ (reserve) but that table over there is free.

3 All the herbs and vegetables ________ (grow) by local farmers.

4 The chefs ________ (cook) some of the meals at your table.

5 The steak ________ (serve) with chips or jacket potatoes.

6 All our desserts ________ (homemade).

7 Most of the staff ________ (speak) English and Japanese.

8 I'm sorry, but we ________ (not accept) credit cards.

4 **Put the words in the box into the correct categories in the table below.**

beans cauliflower diner peas snack bar beef chef duck pork soup ~~café~~ chicken lamb potatoes starter canteen cook main course restaurant waiter carrots dessert manager side dish waitress

places to eat	meat	vegetables	staff	parts of a meal
café				

5 **Complete these sentences. Use one word from exercise 4 in each gap.**

a I asked the [1] ________ to bring us the menu but he forgot.

b I think I'll have tomato soup as a [2] ________ and roast duck as the [3] ________ ________.

c I don't like the food in the office [4] ________ so I usually buy a sandwich or a hamburger from the [5] ________ ________ on the corner.

d This soup is cold. Could you take it back to the kitchen and ask the [6] ________ to heat it up.

1 22 Look at the communication styles a–c, below. Then listen and match the correct communication style to each conversation 1–3.

a
Interrupting is rude. The speakers usually wait until someone has finished speaking before they say something.

b
Interrupting is acceptable and it is important to show you are involved. Sometimes more than one speaker says something at the same time.

c
The speakers pass the topic to one another quickly and everyone is expected to say something. Interrupting is OK.

Conversation 1 ☐
Conversation 2 ☐
Conversation 3 ☐

2 23 What were the questions in the first conversation? Complete the conversation. Put the words in brackets in the correct order. Then listen again and check.

Conversation 1

A: We're going skiing in Switzerland next month.

B: Are you? You'll love it. 1 ____________________? (skied/ Have/before/you)

A: No, this will be my first time. Tim's going to teach me.

C: Really? 2 ____________________? (When/Tim/ski/did/ learn to)

A: He learnt to ski when was in Finland. He …

C: Ah, yes, of course, I forgot Tim stayed at Turku University.

B: 3 ____________________? (a good/he/Is/skier)

A: Ha! I don't know but he says he is.

C: Well, make sure he doesn't make you ski down the Matterhorn on your first day.

3 24 Put the second conversation in the correct order. Then listen again and check.

Conversation 2

I see you are both experts on the area. Can you recommend any restaurants there? ☐

Ah yes, that is a very nice area for skiing. My husband, Klaus, and I went skiing there several times before we got married. ☐

We're going skiing in Switzerland next month. We've booked a room at a guest house in the canton of Valais. ☐

Yes, we're staying in Bagnes. Do you know it? ☐

Yes, there was a very good one, but I'm afraid I can't remember the name of it now. I'll have to ask Klaus. ☐

The skiing conditions are usually very good there in March. Are you staying near Verbier? ☐

Yes, I know it very well. It's in the valley. It's only a ten-minute drive from Verbier. ☐

4 25 Listen to conversation 3 again. Do the speakers develop the conversation by asking questions or by changing the topic?

5 Develop and complete this conversation by asking questions.

A: I'm going skiing next month.

B: ____________________?

A: No, it's my first time.

B: ____________________?

A: Zermatt in Switzerland.

B: Oh, it's wonderful there. ____________________?

A: Yes, we're staying in a lovely hotel right in the town centre.

B: ____________________?

A: Just ten days. We'd like to stay longer, but Chris has to be back at work on the 7th.

1 The information about two festivals, The Running of the Bulls in Spain and the Lantern Festival in China, has been muddled up. Read the article and underline the sentences which are about The Running of the Bulls.

The Festival of San Fermin takes place in the old part of Pamplona, Spain from 6th –14th July every year. Its most famous event is The Running of the Bulls. The Lantern Festival takes place on the fifteenth day of the first month of the Chinese calendar. The festival dates back to the thirteenth century but the 825-metre route that is run today began when the bullring was built in 1844. The run begins at 8:00 a.m. when a rocket is lit. Emperor Wudi of the Han Dynasty declared it as one of the most important festivals in 104 BC. During the festival children go out at night with paper lanterns. It is a dangerous festival: since 1924, 14 people have been killed and over 200 have been badly injured. The organizers hand out information (with safety tips) before the event. The night is full of bright colours and lights. Some of the lanterns have riddles* inside them which can be pulled out and read. If the reader knows the answer, they win a little prize. When the bulls have entered the ring, young cows are then released into the arena. Another important part of the festival is eating sweet rice dumplings* called *Yuan Xiao*. Each area has its own special way of making them.

riddles = questions that are often confusing and have funny or clever answers
rice dumplings = round lumps of rice mixed with water and cooked in boiling water

A The San Fermin festival showing bulls and people running through the streets

B Photo of Chinese lanterns

2 Complete this article about another festival that takes place in Rajasthan, India every year. Put the verbs in brackets in the correct form.

The Elephant Festival

The Elephant Festival is part of the ancient spring festival of Holi. It 1 ________ (hold) every year in Jaipur, the capital of Rajasthan, India.

The elephants 2 ________ (paint) and decorated from head to toe with beautiful jewellery and there is a 'beauty' competition where experts and tourists 3 ________ (decide) on the best decorated elephant. During the festival elephant polo* 4 ________ (play) and there are also races and a tug-of-war* competition between ten people and an elephant. Musicians 5 ________ (play) traditional music and everybody 6 ________ (dance) in the famous Chaugan stadium.

polo = a game played between two teams of players who normally ride on horses and hit a small ball with long-handled wooden hammers
tug-of-war = a contest between two teams who pull opposite ends of a rope against each other

Politely does it

A -ing forms

Q&A

1 How good are your meeting manners? Answer the questions in this quiz and find out.

1 You have an interesting new idea and you want to set up a meeting to discuss it. Is it OK to send an email saying that the meeting is at 4:00 p.m. tomorrow?

- **a** Yes, if you are the boss, you can decide where and when to meet.
- **b** No, giving people so little time means some people may not be able to come.
- **c** Holding meetings in the afternoon is always a good idea.

2 You are meeting in the largest meeting room in your company. It seats 25 people.

- **a** You should invite at least 20 people.
- **b** Send out an invitation to 30–35 people because some people won't have time to come.
- **c** Only invite people who need to be there.

3 Some people like leaving their phones on in meetings. What will you do?

- **a** Tell the participants to leave their phones outside.
- **b** It's OK as long as the call is connected with business.
- **c** It's OK if the phone is switched to vibrate*. They can leave the room if it's really important.

vibrate = shake quickly and continuously with very small movements

4 In the meeting you remember you have forgotten to send an important email to your boss.

- **a** Writing the email in the meeting would be rude. You should do it as soon as the meeting is over.
- **b** Leave the meeting and write the email from your office.
- **c** Switch on your laptop or smart phone and quickly write the message in the meeting.

5 Someone has just given a good presentation. How can you show it was good?

- **a** by banging your hand on the table
- **b** by clapping
- **c** There is no right way. Some cultures will clap; others may bang their hands on the table.

6 You have discussed the points you wanted to talk about. How should you finish the meeting?

- **a** Tell the participants they had amazing ideas even if they didn't.
- **b** Thank everyone for coming, summarize what was agreed and what has to be done now.
- **c** Invite everyone to chat for five minutes, e.g. about the weather, what they enjoy doing, their holiday plans, etc.

2 Look at the quiz again. Find two examples of each of the following.

An *-ing* form …

1 as an adjective.

an interesting new idea ____________

2 as the subject of a sentence.

____________ ____________

3 after a verb showing you like or dislike something.

____________ ____________

3 Complete these sentences. Use one verb from the box in the correct form in each gap.

talk arrive see mix invite give

1 Peruvians don't mind their guests ________ 30 minutes late for a party.

2 Americans seem to enjoy ________ about their jobs and how much money they earn.

3 In Spain, people aren't keen on ________ guests to their homes but if they do, it indicates you are a very good friend.

4 The French don't like ________ their business with pleasure so you should avoid talking about business when you are socializing with them.

5 Russians like ________ small presents, such as flowers or chocolates to their hosts.

6 Keep both your feet on the ground in Egypt. Egyptians don't like ________ the bottom of someone's shoes; showing someone the bottom of your shoe is considered to be insulting.

1 26 Listen to two people talking about a holiday in Turkey and decide if the statements are true (T) or false (F).

1 Pete thinks Turkey is one of the most interesting countries he's ever been to. ☐

2 Pete thinks that Turkish people are very friendly and hospitable. ☐

3 Bridget was embarrassed by Pete's behaviour in a restaurant. ☐

4 Rob is amazed that someone they didn't know paid for Pete and Bridget's meal. ☐

5 Pete and Bridget had a terrible experience in a park. ☐

6 Pete and Bridget went to an underground city. ☐

2 Complete this article about hospitality in different parts of the world. Write the correct form of the words in brackets.

1 ☐
Guests should not be ________ (surprise) at being taken to a restaurant because homes are often small. If a guest is staying the night, they may also be allowed to take the first bath. Unlike Western hospitality styles the host will try to look busy and leave the guest with the feeling that everything is being done to make them feel ________ (relax) and at ease.

2 ☐
The people here like giving and receiving gifts and you are expected to give your host a gift if you are invited to their home. Your host may even be ________ (insult) if you don't bring a small gift with you. Flowers are normally only given to women. An expensive bottle of wine also makes a good gift here but avoid buying vodka as a gift. Whatever gift you decide to buy, make sure it is ________ (interest).

3 ☐
The people here are usually informal so don't be ________ (shock) if people call you by your first name. It is common to greet someone with 'G'day' or 'G'day, mate'. It is common to invite guests to your home for a barbecue. When you are eating hold your fork in your left hand and your knife in your right hand. Kangaroo meat is considered a delicacy but you may be ________ (surprise) to know that a lot of people living there have never tried it.

3 Look at the texts in exercise 2 again and match them to the correct countries a–c below.

A Australia

B Japan

C Russia

4 Complete these sentences. Choose the correct form of the adjectives in *italics*.

1 My next-door neighbour is *interested / interesting* in steam engines.

2 His presentation went on for ages and it was really *bored / boring*.

3 Would you be *embarrassed / embarrassing* if you were voted employee of the year?

4 The film won three Oscars but I thought it was rather *disappointed / disappointing*.

5 I was totally *exhausted / exhausting* after running that marathon.

6 I'm sorry I wasn't *concentrated / concentrating*. What did you say the problem was?

1 Read this article about paying compliments at work and decide if the statements are true (T) or false (F).

Paying compliments at work works

Paying compliments at work has never been more important than it is today … not because people expect them but because they don't expect them. Most of us are more interested in what *we* are doing. We don't take the time to compliment others about the work they're doing.

Most of us expect the boss to tell us we have done a good job from time to time but have you ever thought about paying one of your co-workers a compliment?

Some studies say people who pay compliments are seen as being smarter and more intelligent.

When you pay someone a compliment is also important. Compliments work best if they are given immediately after someone does something well. The longer you wait before giving praise, the less effective it is.

Should you praise your boss? The answer is yes but be careful and make sure your compliments are not too obvious or too frequent.

The old saying, *'Flattery will get you nowhere'*, isn't true. If you flatter and compliment your colleagues, they will respect you and this will help you to get to where you want to be.

1 People don't expect to be paid compliments very often at work. ☐

2 Most people don't expect their boss to praise them. ☐

3 Some studies show that if you pay compliments people will think you are more intelligent. ☐

4 The sooner you pay someone a compliment, the better. ☐

5 It is not a good idea to compliment your boss too often. ☐

6 People won't respect you if you compliment them at work. ☐

2 Match compliments 1–6 with the correct situations a–f.

1 That was a really interesting talk.

2 It really suits you. You look great.

3 It smells absolutely delicious.

4 You always have such great ideas.

5 I really like the way you've decorated this room.

6 I don't know what I would have done without your help. You're so kind.

a Someone has just suggested a solution to a problem.

b Someone looked after you for a few days while you were ill.

c Someone has just had their hair cut.

d Someone is showing you around their house.

e Someone has just finished giving a presentation.

f You are having dinner at someone's home.

3 Complete these compliments. Write the missing letters.

1 Thanks for inviting me. It was a br_ll_ _nt party.

2 That dress makes you l_ _k ten years younger.

3 Blue really s_ _ts you.

4 That's a w_nd_rf_l idea. Why didn't I think of that?

5 What a b_ _ _t_f_l house you have.

6 The photos you took of our wedding are f_nt_st_c. You're so t_l_nt_d.

7 That aftershave you're wearing smells r_ _lly r_c_.

8 This cake is _bs_l_t_ly d_l_c_ _ _s.

1 What is the best thing to say in these situations? Choose the best answers.

1 You are picking up an old school friend from the station.

a It's great to see you again. How are you?

b It's nice to meet you. How do you do?

c It is always a great pleasure to see you. Can I give you a lift?

2 You are giving a party. One of your colleagues is with her husband. You have never met him.

a Mr Peterson, it's nice to meet you.

b Mr David Peterson, how are you?

c Hello Dave. I'm glad you could come.

3 You have invited some guests to your home. You want to tell them that they don't have to ask you for the biscuits and coffee on the table.

a Serve yourselves please.

b Please help yourselves.

c Please take, don't ask.

4 You have invited some guests to your home and want to make them feel relaxed.

a Please feel free to take anything.

b My home is yours.

c Please make yourselves at home.

5 Your guest has just arrived at your home. He is wearing a thick, heavy coat.

a Can I take your coat?

b You must be hot in that coat. Do you want me to open the window?

c Please feel free to remove your coat.

6 Your guests are leaving.

a It's nice to see you.

b Now it's our turn to visit you.

c It was lovely having you.

2 Who would say these things, the host (H), the guest (G) or both (B)?

1	Thanks for inviting me.	G
2	Hi, it's great to have you with us.	
3	Please take a seat.	
4	It's lovely to see you again.	
5	These biscuits are nice. Are they homemade?	
6	What a fantastic view.	
7	Would you like some more?	
8	We must try to see each other more often in future.	

3 27 Complete this conversation. Use one phrase from the box in each gap. Then listen and check.

> **a** You were very lucky **b** What a fantastic view you have from here. **c** Thanks **d** It's lovely to see you, too. **e** Anyway, do come in **f** make yourself at home and **g** Would you like anything to drink? **h** These are for you.

Celia: Tony, it's lovely to see you again. How are you?

Tony: Fine thanks. 1 _______. How are you settling in to the new house?

Celia: Oh, just fine. 2 _______ and give me your coat. I don't think you've seen the house yet, have you?

Tony: No, the last time I saw you was when you were thinking about buying it. It's in a lovely area. 3 _______ to find such a lovely old house.

Celia: Yes, and the price was just right. I said I couldn't afford more than £250,000 and I managed to get the old owner to accept £245,000. Anyway, come through to the living room …

Tony: Thanks. 4 _______.

Celia: Oh, Tony, they're beautiful. You shouldn't have.

Tony: Don't be silly. It's just a little something … Wow! 5 _______.

Celia: Yes, it's lovely. On a clear day we can even see the coast. 6 _______ A cup of tea, coffee, or a fruit juice?

Tony: Oh, a cup of tea would be lovely, thanks.

Celia: OK, well, 7 _______ help yourself to the biscuits.

Tony: 8 _______.

Celia: I'll just put the kettle on.

14

A Present perfect
B Present perfect vs past simple
C **Communication strategies** Public speaking
D **Interaction** Job interviews

Career moves

A Present perfect

1 Read this article and decide if the statements are true (T) or false (F).

The Most Unusual Job in the World?

King Charles II said that there must always be six ravens* at the Tower of London, otherwise the kingdom of England would be destroyed. So for more that 350 years there have been ravens at the Tower and also Ravenmasters to look after them.

Derrick Coyle has worked with the ravens since he left the army when he was 39. He became a Ravenmaster's assistant two months later. He has had the top job of Ravenmaster for over ten years now.

He feeds the birds in the morning, at lunchtime and in the evening but they don't always behave themselves and sometimes he has to 'dismiss' them for bad behaviour. In 1986 a raven called George had to be moved to a zoo in Wales for damaging TV aerials.

Another task the Ravenmaster has is running a breeding programme*. Since 1987 the Tower has bred more than 17 ravens.

In 1995 the Queen presented Derrick with the Royal Victorian Medal for his work.

Derrick is proud of his job. After all he says, 'Who else can say they are a Ravenmaster?'

raven = a large, black bird
breeding programme = to keep animals in order to produce babies

1 There have been ravens at the Tower of London since Charles II was king. ☐

2 Derrick Coyle started work at the Tower of London when he was 30. ☐

3 Derrick has been the Ravenmaster for more than ten years. ☐

4 Derrick has moved at least one raven to another location since he started working at the Tower. ☐

5 The Tower bred 17 chicks in 1987. ☐

6 The Queen gave Derrick a medal. He has had the medal since 1995. ☐

2 Read about Sir Alan Sugar's career and put the verbs in brackets into the present perfect or past simple.

Sir Alan Michael Sugar 1 __left__ (leave) school when he 2 _______ (be) 16 and 3 _______ (start) selling products such as cigarette lighters and cheap electrical goods out of a van he 4 _______ (buy) with his savings of £100.

Sir Alan 5 _______ (set up) the electronics company Amstrad in 1968, in the same year he 6 _______ (marry) his wife, Ann. He is now a multi-millionaire and has an estimated £830 million.

Since 2005 Sugar 7 _______ (star) in the reality TV show *The Apprentice*. There 8 _______ (be) five series so far and Sugar 9 _______ (be) the boss in each since the series began. This means he has to fire a candidate* every week.

'You're fired' 10 _______ now _______ (became) Alan Sugar's catchphrase* in both the US and the UK.

candidate = someone who is competing in a competition or has applied for a job
catchphrase = a popular word or phrase that people use

B Present perfect vs past simple

1 28 **Listen to the conversation and answer these questions.**

1 Have David and Sue seen each other in the last few months?

2 Who does David work for now?

3 How long has David been with SoftX?

4 How long has Sue been with Patchwork Communications?

5 How long has Carlos had his business?

6 When did Carlos' company lose a major client?

2 **Listen again and complete the conversation.**

a Yes, that's right … Hey! Sue, Sue Yates. I [1] ________ you for years.

b Yes, after I [2] ________ Kennedy's, I joined SoftX. I [3] ________ with them for about ten years.

c Patchwork Communications. I'm their sales manager. I've been with them [4] ________ I married Carlos and we moved to San Diego.

d His company develops software for mobile phones. He set it up [5] ________ but he [6] ________ a major client last year.

3 **Complete these sentences. Use *for* or *since* in each gap.**

1 I haven't seen Luigi __*for*__ ages. How is he?

2 We've lived here ________ Pete got a job with Brighton & Hove City Council.

3 I lived in London ________ six years before I moved to New York.

4 I haven't seen Ian ________ 2007 when he left the company.

5 He's been the team leader ________ about six months.

6 I haven't been on any business trips to the USA ________ a long time.

7 We've been very successful ________ we opened a store in China.

8 She worked at a law firm as an intern ________ six months.

4 **Each sentence contains one mistake. In each sentence, find the mistake and correct it.**

1 I have wanted to go to New Zealand ~~for~~ *since* I saw a documentary about it.

2 I have been to university from 2002 – 2005.

3 We have lived in this house since five years.

4 I have had my first car for five years and then I bought a motorbike.

5 Have you ever went to Canada?

6 Tom is working here for about six months.

5 **Look at these timelines. Then reorder the words to make correct sentences in the present perfect or past simple.**

1 since/Harry/working for/has been/1999/Texas Instruments

____.

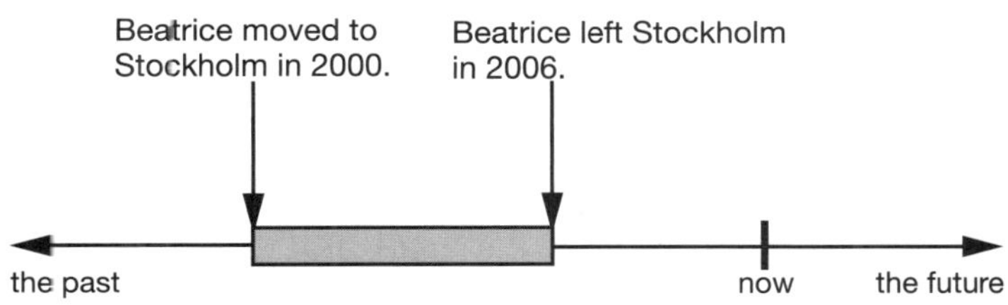

3 lived in/six years/Beatrice/Stockholm/for

____.

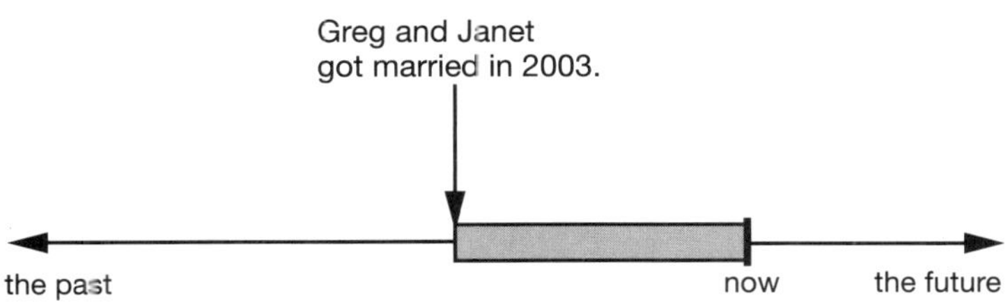

2 have been/Greg and Janet/since/married/2003

____.

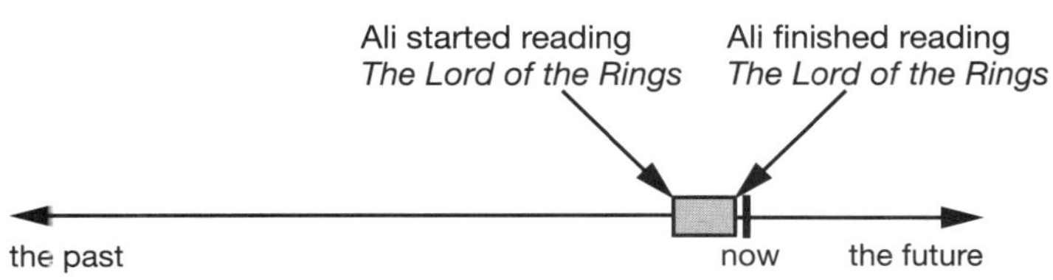

4 read/*The Lord of the Rings*/has/Ali/just

____.

1 Read this article with tips about giving a presentation to an international audience and answer the questions.

Speaking to International Audiences

When you give a presentation to an international audience, remember that what works in your country may not work in other cultures.

Starting your presentation with a joke may be OK in some cultures, but people from other cultures may think it is unnecessary or even rude.

Native English speakers often forget to speak slowly, clearly and to use simple language that non-native speakers will be able to understand. The same is true when experts give presentations: they sometimes forget that people may not understand specialized words. Watch your audience carefully – if you think that some of them do not understand, stop and try to make that point clearer.

European and Japanese audiences expect the speaker to give them much more background and details than an American or Canadian audience, who will be more interested in the big picture and finding out what the bottom line is.

It is common for the audience to clap at the end of a presentation, but that is not universal; people from some countries bang their hands on the table to thank the speaker.

So remember: what is right in your culture is not necessarily right in someone else's.

1 Is telling a joke at the start of a presentation always a good idea?

2 Why is it often difficult to understand native English speakers?

3 What do experts sometimes forget?

4 Why should you watch your audience carefully?

5 Are American audiences more interested in details than European or Japanese audiences?

6 In some cultures do people bang their hands on the table if they don't like a presentation?

2 29 Listen to the beginnings of five presentations and decide whether these statements are true (T) or false (F).

1 The speaker in presentation 1 starts by telling the audience a surprising fact or statistic. ▢

2 The speaker in presentation 2 begins the presentation with a short joke. ▢

3 The speaker in presentation 3 is factual. ▢

4 The speaker in presentation 4 starts by asking the audience to think about a problem. ▢

5 The speaker in presentation 5 tells the audience a story about something that has happened to him. ▢

3 Match sentence halves 1–8 with a–h to make beginnings of presentations.

1 I remember when	**a** how many millions of dollars a year are lost because of shoplifting?
2 Have you ever wondered	**b** on the way to the presentation this morning
3 Did you know that	**c** telling you something about our activities in the USA.
4 Imagine for a second	**d** I first started work.
5 I'd like to start by	**e** that a computer was developed that was more intelligent than man.
6 Something funny happened to me	**f** almost 17,000 people live on every km² of Monaco?
7 Albert Einstein once said:	**g** protect the environment?
8 Are you doing enough to help	**h** 'Imagination is more important than knowledge.'

1 Find 16 words that are connected to work. They are written horizontally, vertically and diagonally.

F	R	O	J	E	C	T	V	S	M
Q	X	T	E	A	M	K	L	Q	A
J	C	R	W	S	Z	L	Y	U	N
Q	I	O	U	Y	I	L	S	A	A
F	J	N	M	K	P	Q	A	L	G
B	O	S	S	P	H	X	L	I	E
B	B	Q	A	Z	A	I	A	F	R
O	F	F	I	C	E	N	R	I	X
Z	X	E	M	P	L	O	Y	E	R
P	O	S	I	T	I	O	N	D	Y

2 Match jobs a–c with skills and personal qualities 1–8.

a Secretary

b Tour guide

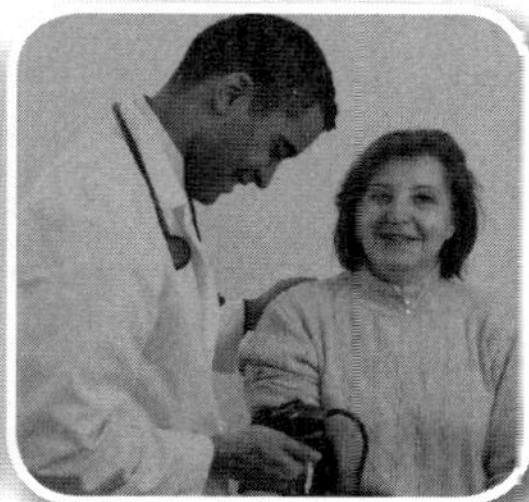
c Doctor

1 knows a lot of interesting things about the area (b) (S)
2 doesn't mind seeing blood ( ) ( )
3 enjoys working with lots of different strangers and foreigners all day ( ) ( )
4 is good at organizing schedules and has excellent telephone skills ( ) ( )
5 is prepared to work at night and whenever there's an emergency ( ) ( )
6 likes walking and working outside in all weather ( ) ( )
7 is good at explaining the results of tests ( ) ( )
8 is good at typing and spelling ( ) ( )

3 Decide if points 1–8 in exercise 2 are skills (S) or personal qualities (P).

4 Match interview questions 1—6 with the correct answer a–f.

1 How long have you worked for British Airways?

2 Can you tell me why you applied for this job?

3 What kind of training have you done since you started work?

4 Have you ever made a serious mistake at work?

5 Tell me about the last project you worked on.

6 Could you tell me what you think your greatest strength is?

a I've done two courses in customer care and a Spanish language course.

b Yes, I helped to train my department to use a new IT program.

c For about 12 years.

d Yes, I think it's being able to work well in a team.

e Yes, I think I have the skills you need and I'm very interested in a new challenge.

f No, never. I've made a few little ones though, but everyone does.

5 Read job adverts 1–3 and the candidates' applications a–c. Then decide which job each candidate is most suitable for.

1 Personal assistant ( )

You are hard-working, flexible and prepared to work around the clock if necessary. You are an expert in Word, Excel and PowerPoint. You speak French and English fluently and are willing to travel.

2 Salesperson ( )

We are looking for someone who is friendly, polite and reliable. Must be prepared to work at weekends. An interest in electronics would be good but it is not a must.

3 Part-time receptionist ( )

SoftGroup is looking for a part-time receptionist for our headquarters in London. Your main responsibilities will be to greet visitors and to deal with security matters. The ideal candidate will have a basic knowledge of four or five languages.

A

.. and as you will see from my CV, I worked as a sales assistant at Mediaworld for 15 years but lost my job when the store closed. I am flexible and good with people. I speak some Spanish and Portuguese.

B

... now that my daughter is at school. I worked as the junior manager at the Bridge hotel until 2005. I really enjoyed working with all the foreign guests we had and organizing trips and tours for them.

C

... and am currently employed as the team assistant but I don't find the work very challenging or interesting. I love travelling and spent a year in Paris when I was studying. I can write about 120 words a minute and ...

15

A Past continuous
B Past simple vs past continuous
C **Communication strategies** Making excuses
D **Interaction** Storytelling

Memories

A Past continuous

1 **Read this article about the founders of the Rolls-Royce Motor Company and decide if the statements are true (T) or false (F).**

How Rolls Met Royce

Henry Royce (1863–1933) and Charles Rolls (1877–1910) came from completely different family backgrounds. Henry Royce's parents were poor and he started working when he was nine years old.

Charles Rolls came from a rich family and was educated at *Eton** and then Cambridge University.

Royce worked for a railway company, and had several jobs before starting his own business making electrical parts. The business did well and he bought his first car in 1901. He thought the car was unreliable and he soon told his colleagues that he would build his own car – and to his high standards.

In 1904 Royce produced his first three cars. He sold one of them to Henry Edmunds, a friend of Charles Rolls. Edmunds showed Rolls his car and arranged the famous meeting between Rolls and Royce. The meeting was a great success and the two of them formed a partnership, Rolls-Royce Ltd, in 1906.

Rolls, who was also interested in aeroplanes, was killed four years later when the tail of the plane he was flying broke off. Sadly, Rolls will also be remembered as being the first Briton to have been killed in a plane crash.

Eton = the most famous public school in England (a public school is a school which is paid for by the parents, not the government)

1 In 1875 Henry Royce was still going to school ☐
2 Royce was building motor cars in 1901. ☐
3 Royce thought the first car he bought was very good and decided to buy more of them. ☐
4 Rolls bought one of the first three cars Royce produced. ☐
5 The first three Rolls-Royce cars were made in 1904 ☐
6 Rolls was driving a car when he died. ☐

2 **Complete the answers to these questions. Use the verbs in brackets in the past continuous.**

1 A: What were you doing when you broke your leg?
B: I _was skiing_ (ski) in the Alps.

2 A: Were you living with your parents when you met Anne?
B: No, I ________ (study) in London then.

3 A: Where was George when I phoned the office this morning?
B: I'm not sure, but I think he ________ (has) a meeting with the sales team.

4 A: What you were doing at this time last week?
B: I had an appointment in Oxford at 2:30 so I ________ (probably drive) down the motorway.

5 A: Why didn't you take an umbrella with you?
B: Because it ________ (not rain) when I left the flat this morning.

6 A: Were you sleeping when I called?
B: No, I ________ (not sleep). I ________ (have) a shower.

1 30 Listen to six situations a–f and then match them to the correct pictures 1–6.

2 Match sentences halves 1–6 with a–f to make correct sentences about the pictures in exercise 1.

1 Jones was sleeping
2 When the man cut his finger,
3 The mountaineer was climbing up a mountain
4 When the waiter tripped,
5 The jogger was running in the park
6 The secretary was trying to change a light bulb

a he was making a sandwich.
b when his boss came into the office.
c when the dog attacked him.
d when she got an electric shock and fell off the chair.
e the couple were reading the menus.
f when his mobile phone rang.

3 Complete these sentences. Put the verbs in brackets in the past simple or past continuous.

1 I ________ (drive) along the highway when I ________ (hear) the news on the radio.

2 I ________ (meet) the man of my dreams when I ________ (stay) with my sister.

3 My wife ________ (break) her leg when we ________ (ski) in Switzerland last winter.

4 Of course I know what I ________ (do) at 5:30 this morning; I ________ (sleep).

5 I ________ (walk) down the road when I ________ (slip) and ________ (fall).

6 My computer ________ (crash) while I ________ (write) you an email!

7 Tom ________ (have) lunch when someone ________ (break into) his office and ________ (steal) his laptop.

8 When the fire alarm ________ (go off), I ________ (be) in a meeting with one of our suppliers.

4 What do these text messages mean? Write the abbreviations as words.

1 CU @8 — *See you at eight.*
2 RU COMING L8R? ________
3 HERE'S A ? 4U ________
4 OK, GR8! CU 2MORO ________
5 NE1 GOING 2 JAKES 2NITE? ________
6 IC UR @WORK ________
7 PLS CALL ME B4 U COME ________
8 THX 4 LETTING ME NO. WILL UB L8? ________

5 Match these replies to the correct text messages in exercise 4.

a YEP, JAY & ME. MAYBE JANE 2. CU THERE (5)
b FRAID I DON'T NO THE ANSWER Y DON'T U ASK PAT? ☐
c NO. WE SHOULD B ON TIME ☐
d OK, TILL 8 THEN ☐
e YEP. WORKING L8 2NITE. HAVE 2 MEET A DEADLINE ☐
f OK. WILL CALL U B4 I LEAVE ☐
g YES, I'LL B WITH U IN AN HR ☐
h TILL 2MORO, THEN ☐

1 Complete these sentences. Choose the correct verb.

1 Thanks for *remembering / reminding* me to buy some flowers for Kate.

2 I *forgot / left* my papers in the conference room.

3 Can you *remember / remind* when they said they would come?

4 I've sent them an email to *remember / remind* them that we need the plans by Monday.

5 Can I use your phone? I'm afraid I *forgot / left* mine.

6 She *forgot / left* her passport at home so she wasn't allowed on the plane.

2 Compete these sentences. Use the correct form of *remember, remind, forget* or *leave* in each gap.

1 Does this photo *remind* you of anyone?

2 Do you think I ________ my bag in the taxi?

3 I must ________ to buy some duty free perfume for Claire when we fly back.

4 Don't ________ anything valuable in the room. Put it in the hotel's safe.

5 Who's that man over there? I talked to him this morning, but I've ________ his name.

6 Ibrahim phoned this morning and ________ me to send him the report.

7 One of the first things I can ________ is my grandparents' house in Sussex.

8 It's strange but I always ________ my umbrella. Last week I ________ it on the train.

3 Match apologies 1–6 with excuses a–f.

1 I'm sorry I'm late.

2 Oops! Sorry! I broke the window!

3 I'm afraid I've spilt some fruit juice over your carpet.

4 I'm sorry I got so angry and shouted at him.

5 I'm afraid I forgot to get that book you wanted.

6 I'm sorry I can't come to your party.

a It was an accident.

b I don't usually behave like that.

c I promise I'll buy it for you tomorrow.

d The traffic was terrible.

e I'm flying to Brazil that weekend.

f I'll pay to have it cleaned of course.

4 Look at excuses a–f in exercise 3 again and answer these questions.

Which excuse(s) …

1 say it was a temporary thing and they don't normally do things like that? (b)

2 explain the person didn't mean to do it? ☐

3 say something else was (partly) responsible? ☐ ☐

4 promise or offer to put things right? ☐ ☐

5 Reorder these words and phrases to make apologies and excuses.

1 I forgot/I'm sorry that/yesterday/to call you/but it was a really busy day.

____

2 I've kept/waiting/you/I'm sorry/The meeting took longer than I thought it would.

____

3 the presentation/I'm afraid/in my office/I left/but I'll call Tom and ask him to email it.

____

4 I won't/I'm afraid/on Saturday/be able to come./I forgot we're visiting Anne's parents.

____

5 you'll have to/your name/remind me of/I'm sorry but /I can never remember names.

____

6 it was my coffee./terribly sorry,/I thought/Oh, I am/Let me buy you another one.

____

6 Complete these conversations. Use one word/phrase from the box in each gap.

a problem **b** I'll buy you a new one. **c** That's **d** I'll send it to you first thing this morning. **e** Forget **f** My train was delayed because of the cold weather.

1 A: I'm sorry I forgot to email you the report yesterday. [1] ________
B: [2] ________ OK. As long as I get it by this afternoon.

2 A: I'm sorry I was late for the meeting. [3] ________
B: No [4] ________. I understand.

3 A: I lost your dictionary. I'm so sorry. I must have left it in the café yesterday morning. [5] ________.
B: [6] ________ it. It was an old dictionary anyway.

1 Match the beginnings of jokes 1–3 with endings a–c.

1 ☐
A judge was punishing three men because they had broken the law. Their sentence was three years in the desert. He told them they could each take one thing with them. The first man decided to take an umbrella so that he could have shade whenever the sun was shining. The second man decided to take a water bottle so that he wouldn't get thirsty. Finally, the third man decided to take a car door.

2 ☐
One day three men were sitting on a train. One of the men looked at the guy sitting next to him and said 'Hey, do you want to hear a really funny joke about accountants?'
The guy next to him replied, 'Well, before you tell that joke, I think you should know that I'm two metres tall, weigh 90 kilos and I'm an accountant. And the guy sitting next to me is two metres tall, weighs 100 kilos and he's an accountant, too. Now, do you still want to tell that joke?'

3 ☐
Two bankers were having a meal in a restaurant when six armed robbers burst in. They lined the guests, including the two bankers, up against a wall, and began taking their wallets, watches, etc. While this was going on banker number one put something into banker number two's hand. Without looking down, banker number two whispered, 'What is this?' Banker number one replied …

a 'It's the $50 I owe you.'

b Later a reporter asked him why he wanted to take that particular object with him.
The man replied, 'If it gets hot, I can roll down the window.'

c The first guy said, 'No, I don't want to have to explain it twice.'

2 31 Listen to a conversation and decide if these statements are true (T) or false (F).

1 The man was thrown out of university for behaving badly. ☐
2 The man crashed his friends' cars. ☐
3 They took the keys and moved the cars when Bob and Pete were dancing. ☐
4 When Bob got to the car he unlocked the driver's door. ☐
5 When Pete came Bob was still trying to open the car. ☐
6 Bob and Pete first thought they had the wrong keys but not the wrong cars. ☐

3 Complete what the man and woman said. Choose the correct form of the verbs. Then listen again and check.

1 I don't believe it. You, wild? What kind of things *did you do? / were you doing*?

2 For example, we once *had / were having* a party at our house.

3 So when they were *dancing / danced* in the living room, we took the keys and moved the cars.

4 When Pete and Bob left, my flatmates and I *were going / went* upstairs …

5 Bob *was still trying / tried* to open the car when Pete arrived.

6 Yes, but they weren't *noticing / didn't notice* they had each other's cars until the next morning.

16

A *would*
B Second conditional
C **Communication strategies** Differences of opinion
D **Interaction** Making your case

The right choice

A *would*

1 32 Listen to a reporter interviewing people about what they would like to do if they won the lottery. Decide if the statements are true (T) or false (F).

Interview 1

1 The man is a regular lottery player. ☐

2 The first thing he would like to do is stop working and cycle around the world. ☐

3 On his return he would like to become a writer. ☐

Interview 2

4 The woman would buy a luxury flat and an expensive car. ☐

5 She wouldn't want a sports car. ☐

6 She thinks that spending the money would be a full-time job. ☐

Interview 3

7 The woman wouldn't do anything with the money. ☐

8 She would give half the money to her family. ☐

9 The woman knows which charity she would give the money to. ☐

2 Listen again and complete the conversations. Write one word or contraction in each gap.

Interview 1

1 And what ________ ________ ________ with all that money if you won?

2 Well, I'd give up work and then ________ ________ ________ ________ around the world. ________ ________ ________ ________ it by bike if I could and then …

Interview 2

3 Excuse me, do you mind if I ask you what ________ ________ ________ ________ with the £32 million if you won it?

4 No, ________ ________ ________ a sports car – an Aston Martin or a Porsche perhaps.

Interview 3

5 Of course, dear. Well, I ________ ________ ________ ________ a thing really.

6 I don't really know yet, dear, but ________ ________ ________ give it to one of those charities where most of the money goes on administration.

3 Complete these sentences using *would* and the words in brackets.

1 I*'d like* (like) a window seat please.

2 ________ (you/prefer to) pay cash or by credit card?

3 I think I ________ (rather have) them in brown, if you have them in this size.

4 I ________ (hate to) fly back without visiting Madame Tussauds.

5 I ________ (rather not) wait for it to be translated into Spanish, let's get it in English.

6 I ________ (not/want to) work for them! Look they only pay £1,300 a month.

7 ________ it ________ (be possible) to have some food brought to our room?

8 I ________ (love to) see it.

1 Read part of an internet forum for unhappy employees. Then complete answers a–c below. Use one phrase from the box in each gap.

> If you took the money
> if one of your colleagues refused to accept the cut
> I would talk to a lawyer

1 ▢	The company I work for has asked the six employees in my department to accept a 50 per cent cut in salary or risk being made redundant. I like the job I have and I wouldn't want any of my colleagues to lose their job but I'm not sure how long I can live on 50 per cent less money. What should I do?
2 ▢	I was fired last week but I wasn't given any reason or warning and my boss told me that if I wasn't happy with the decision, I would have to go to court. I'm not sure what to do. If I went to court and won, I wouldn't want to work for the company again.
3 ▢	My company has offered me six months' salary to leave. I like my job, but if I don't take the money, maybe they will make me redundant for nothing. What would you do if you were me?
a	If this happened to me, I would feel very angry. If you feel you were unfairly dismissed, ____________________.
b	____________________, how long do you think you would need to find another job? Ask yourself what would happen if you accepted the deal but didn't find a job for the next six months.
c	This is a difficult question and I can understand your dilemma. What do you think would happen ____________________? I would wait to see what your colleagues decide to do.

2 Match questions 1–3 with answers a–c in exercise 1.

3 Look at questions 1–3 and answers a–c in exercise 1 again and decide if these statement are true (T) or false (F).

Problem 1

1 If the employees don't accept salary cuts, they will all be fired. ▢

2 The forum writer thinks the person with this problem should quit their job. ▢

Problem 2

3 The person who was fired thinks if he won the court case, he would still go back to the company. ▢

4 The forum writer advises getting legal advice. ▢

Problem 3

5 The person doesn't know whether to accept the money or not. ▢

6 The forum writer thinks the best thing to do is to accept the money. ▢

4 33 Complete this interview. Put the verbs in brackets in the correct form. Then listen and check.

Interviewer:	So, tell me, what you would [1] ________ (take) with you to a desert island.
Sam:	Erm … I'd [2] ________ (take) my mobile phone, some make-up, and … lots of pizzas.
Interviewer:	But if you [3] ________ (be) on a desert island, a mobile phone wouldn't [4] ________ (work). There wouldn't be a signal.
Sam:	That doesn't matter. If there [5] ________ (not be) a signal, I'd just [6] ________ (play) games on it.
Interviewer:	And why would you [7] ________ (need) make-up? You'd [8] ________ (be) alone on the island.
Sam:	Ah, but if a ship [9] ________ (rescue) me, I'd [10] ________ (want) to look nice.
Interviewer:	OK. And all the pizzas?
Sam:	Simple. I love pizza.

1 Complete these expressions. Choose *say* or *tell*.

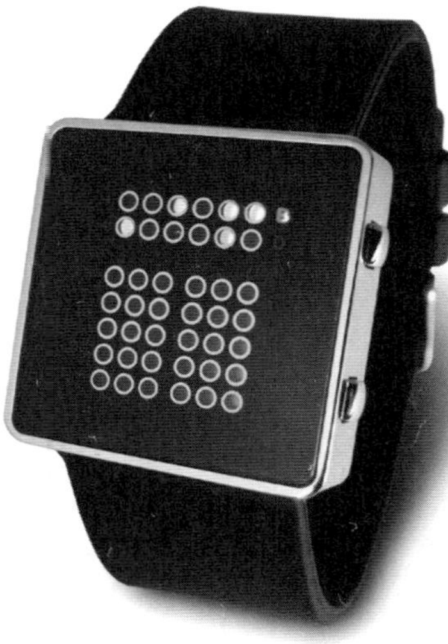

1 How do you *say* / *tell* the time with that watch?

2 Tom, are you OK? Please *say* / *tell* something.

3 I don't think he was *saying* / *telling* the truth.

4 What are you trying to *say* / *tell*?

5 I can't *say* / *tell* the difference. They look exactly the same to me.

6 I'm not very good at *saying* / *telling* jokes.

2 Complete these sentences. Use the correct form of *say* or *tell* in each gap.

1 David ___*said*___ he would meet us at the station at six o'clock.

2 Excuse me, could you ________ me where the post office is?

3 Please ________ hello to Sarah for me when you see her.

4 I ________ you to back those files up yesterday!

5 I'm afraid I can't ________ you that over the phone.

6 What do you think he will ________ if I ask him for a pay rise?

3 34 Put this conversation in the correct order. Then listen and check.

B: Do you really think we'll find a better offer? ☐

A: I'm not happy with our paper supplier. I think we should look for a new one. ☐

B: No, I don't think we should. They've always been reliable. ☐

A: Well, … maybe you're right but I still think we should ask some other companies to send us offers. ☐

A: Well, I'm afraid I think their paper's too expensive. ☐

B: What's the problem? We've used them for years and we've never had any trouble with them. ☐

A: Yes, but we could try to find a cheaper supplier of the paper we use now. ☐

B: Yes, but we've tried using cheaper paper and it jammed the photocopiers. ☐

A: Yes, I think we will. ☐

4 Complete this dialogue. Use one phrase from the box in each gap.

a Yes, but you **b** We could **c** Don't you think **d** Well, erm… can **e** Do we have to **f** I'm afraid

A: I'd like to go to Iceland for a holiday this year.

B: Iceland? [1] ________ you go swimming there? The water must be freezing.

A: The sea's cold but there are lots of hot springs there.

B: [2] ________ probably have to pay a lot of money to use them. I think we should go to somewhere warm and sunny where we can sunbathe and swim in the sea for free.

A: [3] ________ go to somewhere hot and sunny again? [4] ________ it's a bit boring lying on the beach all day?

B: [5] ________ lying on the beach doing nothing is my idea of a perfect holiday.

A: Well, I've got a good idea. [6] ________ fly to Iceland this summer and go for a two-week holiday in the Bahamas in the winter.

B: Hmm … actually, that sounds like a good idea.

Hot springs

1 Complete this crossword puzzle.

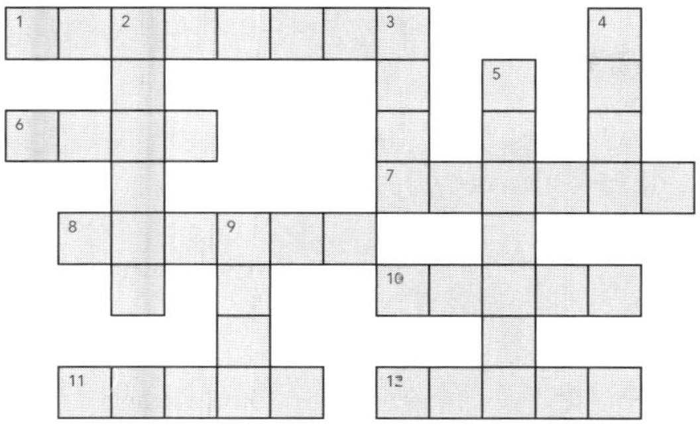

Across

1 The plane crashed into a forest but luckily all the passengers and crew ________. (8)

6 The coastguard Paul Waugh put his life at ________ when he climbed down the cliff to rescue Faye Harrison. (4)

7 Coastguards are people who help sailors, fishermen and swimmers when they are in ________. (6)

8 This museum is open to the ________ from 9:00 a.m. to 5:30 p.m. (6)

10 A high piece of land or rock with a very steep side, usually next to the sea (5)

11 Lifeguards ________ the lives of dozens of people last year. (5)

12 How you would feel if someone did something to you that was unfair or unacceptable. (5)

Down

2 To save someone who is in a dangerous situation (6)

3 You are lucky to be alive! You could have ________ when that gas bottle exploded. (4)

4 The opposite of *dangerous* (4)

5 If you hold onto something with your hands but there is nothing to support your feet, you are ________. (7)

9 You're my hero! You saved my ________. (4)

QUIZ

2 How good are your survival skills? Do this quiz and find out.

1 Which of these three things could you use to start a fire?
- **a** water
- **b** snow
- **c** ice

2 What would be the most important thing to have if you were in a survival situation?
- **a** food
- **b** water
- **c** a knife

3 How long do you think you could survive if you didn't have anything to eat?
- **a** about a week
- **b** about three weeks
- **c** about six weeks

4 You were on a small aeroplane when it crashed into a mountain. Nobody is seriously injured. What should you do?
- **a** stay near the plane and wait to be rescued
- **b** get away from the plane as quickly as you can because it could explode
- **c** climb down the mountain and hope to find help

5 If you were lost in a forest or jungle, what would the safest thing to eat be?
- **a** fruit and berries
- **b** plants
- **c** insects

6 You are in the forest when you meet a large bear. What would be the best thing to do?
- **a** don't look at the bear and walk away slowly
- **b** run away as fast as you can
- **c** lie on the ground and pretend to be dead

Audio scripts

1A, page 4, Exercise 1

1

Christof: Hi. My name's Christof and I'm from Germany. I'm working as an intern in the New York office of an international bank. This is my first time in New York and I love it because it's so exciting and lively. The only problem is I have to work much longer hours here. I'm not so keen on that! But that's normal in the US. I hope I have a chance to visit Chandrika while I'm here, she's a friend of the family.

2

Chandrika: Hello, my name's Chandrika. I come from India. I'm working as an IT manager in Vancouver at the moment. Vancouver is a fantastic place, I really like the people – they're so friendly but I don't like the weather – it's too cold in winter. I rarely stay in one country longer than a year. I'm off to Australia next. I have friends there.

3

Jenny: How's it going? I'm Jenny, a student from Australia. This is my gap year and I'm travelling around the world by plane and train. I love to travel. I sometimes miss home, but I phone home regularly. Right now, I'm checking out London, I love the shops but I don't like the weather much – it rains all the time. For my next trip, I want to visit Chandrika when she's back in India.

4

Chun Hua: I'm an MBA student in Munich. My name is Chun Hua. I come from Chang Chung, a city of five million people in China. I work hard, which I enjoy, and I get up at 7 a.m. every day to go to the university library. I like Berlin because it's a very clean city but unfortunately the food is not so good here. I know Christof from the university. I think he's in the US at the moment.

1C, page 6, Exercises 5 and 6

1

A = Man, **B** = Woman

A: Do you mind if I borrow your car this evening?

B: Sorry. I'm afraid I need it myself this evening.

2

A = Man, **B** = Woman

A: Could I have another piece of cake?

B: Please help yourself.

3

A = Woman 1, **B** = Woman 2

A: Do you mind if I open the window? It's so hot in here.

B: No, not at all. Go ahead.

4

A = Woman, **B** = Man

A: May I use your laptop for ten minutes?

B: Feel free.

5

A = Woman, **B** = Man

A: Do you mind if I leave half an hour early today?

B: Not at all.

6

A = Man, **B** = Woman

A: Could I borrow your dictionary?

B: Sure. Here you are.

2A, page 8, Exercises 1 and 2

1

C = Cathy Wong, **R** = Richard Willis

C: Good morning, BRD Softlab. My name's Cathy. How can I help you?

R: Oh, hello. My name's Richard Willis. I'm having problems installing a program, Money-Wise …

C: Which version of Money-Wise do you use, Mr Willis?

R: The latest version, eight point oh.

C: OK, Mr Willis. Just a moment. I'll put you through to technical support.

R: Thank you.

2

C = Chris, **K** = Ken

C: Oh no! Not again.

K: What's the matter, Chris?

C: The computer's frozen. It's the third time this morning and the last time it happened I lost an hour's work.

K: Really? How annoying. I'm going to the IT department for a meeting in a minute so I'll ask one of the technicians to come and have a look at your PC.

C: Thanks, Ken. That'd be great.

3

A = Woman 1, **B** = Woman 2

A: … and I'm sure it's a hardware problem.

B: OK, I'll send someone round, but could you also check that it really is a hardware problem by running a diagnostics test?

A: Erm … a diagnostics test? How do I do that?

B: Oh, it's very simple. If you have a couple of minutes, I'll tell you what you have to do … or I'll call you back a bit later and …

A: Oh no, I have time. Let's do it now …

4

K = Kate, **B** = Becky

B: Hi Kate, I'm calling about the report. I'm afraid I can't open the file you sent me.

K: Hi Becky. OK, I'll resend it.

B: I don't think that will help, Kate.

K: Why not?

B: I think you're using a newer version of the program. I only have version five point oh.

K: Ah, yes that could be the problem. I'll save the file in version five point oh then.

B: Thanks. I'll get back to you if I still can't open it.

2B, page 9, Exercise 3

1

… s dot trotter at mail dot com

2

… Maria underscore Sanchez at California hyphen gardens dot org

3

… www dot house and home, all one word, dot co dot u k

4

… www dot blogs dot ct dot com forward slash deartom, all one word

5

… www dot ctvgroup, all one word dot com forward slash news forward slash latest dot php

6

… j dot maier – that's m, a, i, e, r – at mattison – that's m, a double t, i, s, o, n – dot a, u

2D, page 11, Exercise 2

H = Heinrich, **G** = Giuseppe

H: Hi Giuseppe. It's Heinrich here.

G: Hello Heinrich. Where are you?

H: I'm still on the train, but I'll be at the station in 20 minutes.

G: OK, I'll come and pick you up.

H: Oh thanks, Giuseppe. That's very kind of you.

G: It's no trouble. I'll be in a red Mini.

H: OK. Looking forward to seeing you.

G: Looking forward to seeing you, too.

3C, page 14, Exercise 1

1

A = Woman 1, **B** = Woman 2

A: Something really silly happened to me today. I forgot where I parked my car!

B: How terrible! What did you do?

A: I spent more than 40 minutes looking for it.

B: You poor thing! At least you found it.

2

A = Man 1, **B** = Man 2

A: I passed my driving test yesterday.

B: That's great! Congratulations! Was it your first test?

A: Yes, it was. And my Dad gave me his old car so I can go where I want now.

B: Brilliant! … Actually, could you give me a lift into town?

3
A = Woman 1, B = Woman 2

A You know I entered that singing competition? Well, I won it!

B Wow! That's fantastic! Were you on TV?

A: Yes, I was. Last Saturday.

B Oh no! I missed it. What a shame.

4
A = Man, B = Woman

A: Someone stole my laptop with my presentation on it.

B: That's terrible. Did you get it back?

A: I'm afraid not. I had to write the presentation again, all those charts and slides.

B: What a nuisance. It must have taken a long time.

4C, page 18, Exercises 1 and 2

1
A = Man, B = Woman

A: I love your new hair style. It looks great.

B: Thanks, I'm glad you like it.

A: Yes, short hair really suits you.

2
A = Man, B = Woman

A: Here's a little something for all the help you've given us.

B: Oh, thank you, they're beautiful but it really isn't necessary.

A: Don't be silly! You're welcome.

3
A = Man, B = Woman

A: I really like your blog. It's full of useful information.

B: Oh, thanks. Sometimes I think my posts are a bit technical.

A: No, not at all – even I can understand them.

4
A = Man, B = Woman

A: Oh no! I've forgotten the cable for the digital projector.

B: No problem. I've got one in my office. I'll get it.

A: Thanks, that's brilliant. You're a lifesaver.

5
A = Woman, B = Man

A: Just let us know what you need from the shops and we'll get it for you

B: Thanks Mary, but are you sure? I don't want you to go to any trouble.

A: Don't be silly. It's no trouble. It's only for a couple of weeks until you're well again.

5A, page 20, Exercises 2 and 3

A = Man 1, B = Man 2, C = Woman

A: We have too many long meetings where we don't decide anything. That usually means we have to have another meeting. People often come late and are not prepared, or the wrong people come to the meeting. I often leave the meeting thinking, 'What a waste of time!' We're going to introduce some changes. We're going to limit meetings to one hour. If we don't make a decision – tough! Also, we're going to hold meetings standing up and not sitting in comfortable chairs. And the meetings are going to start on time!

B: We get so many emails with really big attachments. We don't have time to read them so most people print them out to read later and put them away in files. Of course most people forget about them and never read them and then throw them away a year later. What a waste! Things are going to change! We're not going to send big attachments. We're going to have one file for all teams and we're going to stop printing everything.

C: We have too many teams and project groups working on similar areas. The teams don't speak to each other and share information. So what are we going to change? We're going to have one person to check all project work. We're going to share information with all teams. And we're not going to have two teams working on the same project.

5C, page 22, Exercises 5 and 6

1
A = Man, B = Woman

A: I'm going to Phil's party this evening. Do you think I could borrow your car?

B: I'm afraid not. I need it myself.

A: No problem. I'll take the bus.

2
A = Woman 1, B = Woman 2

A: I've got my English test tomorrow and I can't find my dictionary anywhere …

B: Do you want to take mine?

A: That would be great. You'll get it back tomorrow.

3
A = Man, B = Woman

A: Mmmmm. That smells fantastic. What are you cooking?

B: Chicken curry. Would you like to stay for dinner?

A: I don't want to be any trouble …

B: No trouble at all. I'll set another place.

A: OK, then. That would be great. Thanks.

4
A = Man 1, B = Man 2

A: Could you help me with this email? I don't know what to write.

B: Yes, of course. Just give me a minute and I'll be right with you.

6B, page 25, Exercise 2

A = Man, B = Woman

A: I see you're interested in the Aptera.

B: Yes, I've never seen anything like it before. It looks like a plane without wings.

A: Yes, you're right, but I'm afraid it can't fly.

B: Is it safe? It looks so light and small.

A: Actually, the car weighs about half as much as a normal car, but it is very safe.

B: Really? That's interesting. What's the top speed?

A: Well, it's certainly not as fast as a sports car, but it has a top speed of 85 miles per hour, so it is fast enough to get you a speeding ticket.

B: What about the fuel consumption? How much fuel does the car need?

A: That's not an easy question to answer. It's a hybrid car, so it runs on gas and electricity. If you drive less than 50 miles, you don't need any gas because you use the battery, but the manufacturer says the car does about 300 miles per gallon.

A: That's amazing! And who makes the car?

B: A company called Aptera Motors. It's a Californian company and Google is one of its investors.

A: Google the search engine people?

B: Yes, that's right.

A: Really? So how much does the car cost? I expect it's expensive.

B: No, this model here only costs $25,000.

6C, page 26, Exercises 3 and 4

A = Man, B = Woman

A: Good afternoon, madam. Can I help you?

B: Yes, I'd like to know a bit more about the red car out there.

A: Ah, the Golf? Well, it's only had one careful owner and no accidents.

B: Yes, it looks as if it's in very good condition.

A: Yes, there's nothing wrong with that car. I'm offering it with a two-year guarantee.

B: Really?

A: Yes, there's been a lot of interest in that car, so if you're thinking of buying it, don't think too long because I can't guarantee that it'll still be for sale tomorrow.

B: OK and you want £12,000 for it?

7A, page 28, Exercise 3

A = Man, N = Mr Neumann

A: So Mr Neumann, could you tell us something about living and working in Germany?

N: Certainly. Let's start with work. You should always shake hands with your work colleagues every day. But you mustn't use first names immediately, only when you know people better.

A: And are there lots of rules in the workplace?

N: We are quite formal at work. You don't have to wear a uniform but you should always dress smartly. Like most cultures you are expected to be punctual and professional. So, for example, for meetings you should arrive on time and you have to switch off your mobile phone.

A: I see. So, what about food? Is it important in Germany?

N: Yes, it is. People like eating out so you should book a table if it's a popular restaurant, but you can sit where you like. You should say 'Guten Appetit' before you start eating. Tipping is obligatory so you must give the waiter a tip of 10 to 15 per cent.

A: I've heard that in Germany people love their cars.

N: Yes, that's true. There's no speed limit on most motorways so you can drive as fast as you like. Of course, you must wear your seat belt or you'll have to pay a fine. Although we love our cars, you can't wash your car outside your house on a Sunday – because your neighbours will complain.

N: Really? That's interesting …

7C, page 30, Exercises 1 and 2

E = Emily, D = Douglas

E: Do you ever sell things on eBay?

D: Yeah, all the time. Why?

E: Well, I've got some old stuff to sell. Can you give me some advice?

D: There's nothing to it. First, you should do some research.

E: Research?

D: Yes. You need to find out what kind of things people want and what prices they're willing to pay for them.

E: I see.

D: After that, you have to find the right category for your items. You can put them in several categories.

E: OK … What else is important?

D: You should include a good photo of your item and write an accurate description. Make sure it's clear, understandable and contains as much detail as possible.

E: Right, so describe everything?

D: That's right. And try not to hide any problems because people will probably complain when they get the item. Next, you should set a low opening price to attract more bidders.

E: Yes, that makes sense.

D: Finally, don't forget to state your shipping fees, but don't make them too high.

E: Right. Well, that seems quite straightforward. Thanks.

7C, page 30, Exercises 4 and 5

1

A = Man, B = Woman

A: So, we've got four separate bins for the household rubbish. Try not to mix them up. Let's start with the yellow one. You put plastic and metal rubbish in that. You need to wash out the plastic containers first.

B: Right.

A: Then there's the blue bin. That's easy, it's only for paper. Next, there's the green bin. You need to put garden rubbish like grass in there. You can also put leftover food in it, but no meat. Don't forget, please.

B: OK. No meat.

A: Finally, you put everything else in the grey bin. OK. Is everything clear?

B: Yes.

A: Great.

2

A = Woman 1, B = Woman 2

A: I'm going to apply for a job at an American company. I want to email the application. I've got the document open. Would you have a look at it and see if it's OK?

B: No, it isn't. Save your application in a new document. You can keep the page layout, but you have to delete a lot of things.

A: What should I delete?

B: Delete your photo.

A: What? No photo?

B: Yes. You can copy your education and paste it in under job experience. Don't forget to put your present job first.

A: OK now?

B: No. Let's go back to the top. Delete your date of birth.

A: Really? Why?

B: Look, just do it and save the changes. And don't forget to highlight the text and click on American English for a spell check.

A: OK. Well … thanks for your help.

B: It needs more work, but I don't have the time now.

3

A = Woman, B = Man

A: Right. First, insert the battery into the battery charger. Don't forget to match up the symbols.

B: Like this?

A: Exactly. Good. Then you need to plug the battery charger into the power outlet. Look at the charge indicator. It lights orange when charging.

B: How long does it take?

A: Good question. It takes about two hours. This light turns green when the charging is complete. Don't forget to remove the battery when it's charged.

B: Right.

A: And finally, try not to charge for longer than 24 hours or you might damage the battery.

B: OK. Thanks.

8A, page 32, Exercises 1 and 2

K = Kate, J = John

K: I bought my grandmother a mobile phone for her birthday, but she doesn't use it. She says it too complicated and the buttons are too small.

J: How old's your gran now, Kate?

K: 70.

J: Yes, well, older people sometimes have problems using modern technology because the designers have included too many features. Have you thought about buying her a mobile phone designed specially for older people?

K: No, I didn't think anyone made phones like that.

J: Oh yes, I bought one for my mother recently. It has big dialling buttons, a large easy to read screen and a red speed-dial button on the back.

K: How does the speed-dial button work?

J: Well, you can programme up to five emergency numbers into the phone. Let's say you have fallen or need help. When you press the speed-dial button, the phone rings the first number. If nobody answers, it rings the next number.

K: Hey, that sounds just like the type of phone my gran needs. Thanks, John.

J: No problem.

K: Has your mother had any trouble using it?

J: No, none. She's been using it for about a month and she says she hasn't even read the manual.

9B, page 37, Exercises 4 and 5

L = Laura, A = Alex

A: Hi Laura. How's the conference going?

L: Oh, hi Alex. It's going great, thanks. I'm travelling back on Saturday morning. What's up?

A: We've got some rescheduling for tomorrow.

L: OK – let me get my diary. So – what's new?

A: Something's come up with the London office so your first appointment at eight o'clock is cancelled. You're having a telephone conference with Frank in New York instead.

L: Sounds good.

A: Your nine o'clock meeting with the new marketing manager is still looking good, but we have no confirmation of your eleven o'clock briefing with the sales team. I'll keep you posted. John wants to speak to you urgently so you're meeting him for a working lunch at twelve. I'm afraid it's the only time available for him.

L: OK. What else?

A: The two o'clock meeting is still on, but you're going to Mike's office as he has appointments all day. At three o'clock you're driving to the airport for your interview with Tony Lee as planned.

L: And what about my five o'clock appointment?

A: I'm postponing that till six o'clock because of traffic on the way back from the airport. That's it for tomorrow.

L: OK. Thanks.

A: See you back in the office.

9C, page 38, Exercises 4 and 5

1

A = Woman, B = Man

A: Are you doing anything special on Saturday?

B: Not really. Why?

A: Well, we're having some people round. Would you like to come?

B: Sounds great. Can I check the time and get back to you?

A: Can you let me know by Friday?

B: Of course.

2

A = Man, B = Woman

A: Have you got any plans for Saturday?

B: Why? What's going on?

A: We're having a small get-together at my house. Can you make it?

B: It's nice of you to think of me. I'd love to come. Thanks.

3

A = Man, B = Woman

A: Would you like to join us for coffee on Sunday afternoon?

B: Oh, I'm afraid I'm completely booked up the whole weekend.

A: No problem. Maybe another time.

10A, page 40, Exercise 1

P = Pat, B = Bob

P: I think this is one of the best office buildings you've shown me so far. How many square metres of space does it have?

B: Just over 1,200 so it would give you a bit of space to expand.

P: Yes, that's important. I don't want to have to move offices for a few years.

B: How many times have you moved so far?

P: Three times in the last seven years.

B: Wow!

P: Yeah … Does the building have enough parking? There didn't seem to be much parking at the front.

B: Well, there's a large car park at the back. I'm not sure how many cars can park there, but I think about 50 and then there is an underground car park for about 200 cars.

P: Well, that's more than enough.

B: Yep, and a parking space doesn't cost much to rent – only £39 a month.

P: OK, so how much would the rent for this office space and, erm … let's say 40 parking spaces cost?

B: Sorry, how many did you say?

P: 40.

B: Just a second … about £28,000 a month.

P: Hmm … OK, well, that's not too bad. It's not as much as I thought you would say. I'll have to think about it.

10B, page 41, Exercises 1 and 2

1

A = Man 1, B = Man 2

A: I'm afraid I'm not very happy with the hotel we're in. It's too far from the beach and another hotel is being built next to it so it's really noisy and dusty.

B: Your hotel is right above the beach …

A: Yes, but now it's a 20-minute walk from the hotel to the beach because we can't use the cliff path. It's too dangerous.

B: Too dangerous?

A: Yes, part of the path fell into the sea after the storm last night. Someone's put a sign up saying the path is closed.

B: And you say it's noisy?

A: Very noisy! They start work on the new hotel at seven in the morning and it's *bang, bang, bang, bang* until ten o'clock at night. It's terrible.

B: OK, Mr Jackson, I'll see if we have a room free at the Pine Beach Hotel. Can I call you back a bit later?

A: Yes, of course, but don't be too long!

2

A = Man 1, B = Man 2

A: We'd like to change the room we're in. Can we have a room on the north side of the hotel?

B: Yes, of course, but our guests usually prefer the south side because of the view of the coastline.

A: Yes, it's a lovely view, but the room gets too hot during the day and it doesn't cool down enough at night, even with the air-conditioning on.

B: Maybe the air-conditioning unit isn't working properly. I'll ask maintenance to check.

A: OK, but we'd still prefer a room on the other side of the hotel.

B: Just a second. Let me check. Well, the Nelson suite is free, but we'd have to charge you another $120 a night.

A: $120! Oh, no, that's too expensive.

B: Well, I've got a room with twin beds that I can offer you for the same price …

A: That's fine. A twin room's good enough. We'll take that.

11C, page 46, Exercises 3 and 4

A = Man, B = Woman

1

A: I'm not sure about CCTV cameras in the staff rest area. Lidl tried it and got very bad publicity.

B: Perhaps it's a better idea to reward staff who report employee theft.

2

A: We could hire a consultant to give us advice on what sort of staff training we need.

B: Training is always worth it.

3

A: All the stores in London have security guards in uniform at the door. They look tough. I'm sure they stop people even thinking about shoplifting.

B: Yes, but they're expensive. Are they really worth it?

4

A: So why don't we just hire more sales staff?

B: And we could specially train them to look out for shoplifters and employee theft.

5

A: Maybe we need to search our sales staff.

B: Yes, but they'll complain to the union and we'll find ourselves in the newspapers, too.

12C, page 50, Exercises 1, 2, 3 and 4

1

A = Woman 1, **B** = Woman 2

C = Woman 3

A: We're going skiing in Switzerland next month.

B: Are you? You'll love it. Have you skied before?

A: No, this will be my first time. Tim's going to teach me.

C: Really? When did Tim learn to ski?

A: He learnt to ski when he was in Finland. He was …

C: Ah, yes, of course, I forgot Tim stayed at Turku University.

B: Is he a good skier?

A: Ha! I don't know, but he says he is.

C: Well, make sure he doesn't make you ski down the Matterhorn on your first day.

2

A = Man 1, **B** = Woman, **C** = Man 2

A: We're going skiing in Switzerland next month. We've booked a room at a guest house in the canton of Valais.

B: Ah yes, that is a very nice area for skiing. My husband, Klaus, and I went skiing there several times before we got married.

C: The skiing conditions are usually very good there in March. Are you staying near Verbier?

A: Yes, we're staying in Bagnes. Do you know it?

C: Yes, I know it very well. It's in the valley. It's only a ten-minute drive from Verbier.

A: I see you are both experts on the area. Can you recommend any restaurants there?

B: Yes, there was a very good one, but I'm afraid I can't remember the name of it now. I'll have to ask Klaus.

3

A = Man 1, **B** = Woman, **C** = Man 2

A: We're going skiing in Switzerland next month. We're …

B: You're going skiing. I don't believe it. You're not?

C: You'll kill yourselves!

A: Yes, I know, but we've …

B: Since when can you ski?

A: … we've organized some lessons with a ski instructor.

B: I hope he's good.

C: My uncle tried skiing once.

A: Your uncle?

B: Which uncle?

A: Your uncle Paolo?

C: No, my uncle Luca.

B: And what happened?

C: Well, he …

A: Did he break anything?

C: Yes, the record for slowest downhill skier of all time!

13B, page 53, Exercise 1

R = Rob, **P** = Pete

R: Hi Pete. How are you? How was your holiday? You were in Turkey, weren't you?

P: Oh, hi Rob. Yes, that's right. It was fantastic. Have you ever been to Turkey?

R: No, I haven't been there yet.

P: Well, you really must go. It's one of the most interesting places I've ever been to and the people are so friendly.

R: Yes, I've heard they're very hospitable.

P: Yes, sometimes it was almost embarrassing.

R: Really? Why?

P: Well, for example one day Bridget and I went to a restaurant and had a three-course meal there. When we asked for the bill, the waiter told us one of the other guests had paid for us.

R: Really? And who was it?

P: We never found out. The waiter told us the guest had left.

R: That's amazing.

P: And another time we were sitting in a park and a family invited us to join their barbecue. Bridget was a bit shocked and tried to think of an excuse, but they insisted. Everyone was so friendly.

R: And did you see a lot of interesting places?

P: Oh yes, we visited an ancient underground city and we saw …

13D, page 55, Exercise 3

C = Celia, **T** = Tony

C: Tony, it's lovely to see you again. How are you?

T: Fine thanks. It's lovely to see you, too. How are you settling in to the new house?

C: Oh, just fine. Anyway, do come in and give me your coat. I don't think you've seen the new house yet, have you?

T: No, the last time I saw you was when you were thinking about buying it. It's in a lovely area. You were very lucky to find such a lovely old house.

C: Yes, and the price was just right. I said I couldn't afford more than £250,000 and I managed to get the old owner to accept 245. Anyway, come through to the living room …

T: Thanks. These are for you.

C: Oh, Tony, they're beautiful. You shouldn't have.

T: Don't be silly. It's just a little something … Wow! What a fantastic view you have from here.

C: Yes, it's lovely. On a clear day we can even see the coast. Would you like anything to drink? A cup of tea, coffee, or a fruit juice?

T: Oh, a cup of tea would be lovely, thanks.

C: OK, well make yourself at home and help yourself to the biscuits.

T: Thanks.

C: I'll just put the kettle on …

14B, page 57, Exercises 1 and 2

S = Sue, **D** = David

S: David? David Archer?

D: Yes, that's right. Hey! Sue. Sue Yates. I haven't seen you for years! It's great to see you again. What are you doing here?

S: I'm checking out what the competition has to offer.

D: I'll have to tell my colleagues on the SoftX stand to be careful what they show you then.

S: Oh I don't think they need to worry. So you work for SoftX now?

D: Yes, after I left Kennedys, I joined SoftX. I've been with them for about ten years. What about you? Who do you work for now?

S: Patchwork Communications. I'm their sales manager. I've been with them since I married Carlos and we moved to San Diego.

D: You and Carlos are married now? I didn't know that. How is he?

S: Oh, he's fine, but his business hasn't been doing very well lately, so …

D: What kind of business does he have?

S: His company develops software for mobile phones. He set it up five years ago, but he lost a major client last year and hasn't found enough new business to make up for that.

D: I see. That's tough. But you're doing OK?

S: Oh yeah, I'm fine. Listen, why don't we get some coffee?

D: Yes, that's a great idea.

14C, page 58, Exercise 2

1

If we took all the cables that have been installed at the airport and laid them end to end, they would go around the world four times. That means we have more than 160,000 kilometres of cable here.

2

I can still remember my first PC, an Amstrad, which I bought in 1985. You may laugh, but it had a lot less memory than this USB stick here and about the only thing you could use it for was as a word processor.

3
OK, so my presentation today is about Web 2.0 and how we can introduce Web 2.0 technologies into classrooms. First, I'd like to look at wikis and then I'll move on to talk a little about Facebook.

4
A funny thing happened to me as I was coming here this morning. I got a call on my cell phone from Dave Samson, your head of IT.

'Hi Dave!' I said.

'Where are you, Bob?' he asked, 'I need to talk to you about data security.'

'Great!' I said, 'Why don't you come to my talk this morning?'

'Can't.' he said. 'My secretary's put me down for some stupid presentation here at the company.'

'When?' I asked.

'10 o'clock' he said.

'OK, well, I'll see you there then. I'm the guy who's giving that stupid presentation.'

5
OK, so imagine someone breaks into your home and steals your PC and your external hard drive with all your files on it. That's ten years' data gone. So is there a way that you can still recover your files? Well, there is. Now, have you ever thought about …

15D, page 63, Exercises 2 and 3

A = Woman, **B** = Man

A: Your sister told me you were almost thrown out of university because of all the practical jokes you played.

B: Oh yes, I was a bit wild when I was a student.

A: I don't believe it. You, wild? What kind of things did you do?

B: Oh, all kinds of crazy things. For example, we once had a party at our house. Two friends came who both had the same colour and type of car – white VW Golfs. So I decided to swap them.

A: Swap them? What do you mean?

B: Change them over. One of the cars was parked opposite our flat and the other one was about 50 metres up the road, so we moved both the cars. We parked Bob's car where Pete's was and Pete's car where Bob's was.

A: But how did you get the keys?

B: That was easy. The keys were in their coats and their coats were hanging in the hall. So when they were dancing in the living room, we took the keys and moved the cars. When we finished we put the keys back in their coats again.

A: So what happened?

B: When Pete and Bob left, my flatmates and I went upstairs to a bedroom where we could see the cars better. It was too dark to see Pete's car, but Bob's car was in front of the flat under a streetlight. When Bob reached the car he tried pressing the key to open the door but of course nothing happened so then he tried putting the key in the keyhole but it didn't fit. He walked round to the other door but he couldn't open that door either.

A: What happened then?

B: Bob was still trying to open the car when Pete arrived. They talked for a few minutes and then Pete tried opening the door with his key and, of course, it worked. So they swapped keys and Pete walked back to the other car.

A: But the other car was Bob's not his!

B: Yes but they didn't notice they had each other's cars until the next morning!

A: Yes, it sounds as if you really were a bit wild.

16A, page 64, Exercises 1 and 2

D = DJ, **J** = Jane, **A** = Man 1

B = Woman 1, **C** = Woman 2

1
D: Welcome back. Well, there's over £30 million in the lottery jackpot this week so we asked reporter Jane Davey to find out what people buying lottery tickets would do if they won.

J: Good morning.

A: Oh, erm, good morning.

J: I see you're playing the lottery this weekend.

A: Yes, that's right. I don't usually play, but there's £32 million in the jackpot this week.

J: And what would you do with all that money if you won?

A: Well, I'd give up work and then I'd like to travel around the world. I'd love to do it by bike if I could and then I'd like to buy a villa somewhere warm and sunny and write about my travels.

J: Well, I wish you lots of luck.

A: Thanks.

2
J: Excuse me, do you mind if I ask you what you'd like to do with the £32 million if you won it?

B: Oh, yeah that would be fantastic! I'd buy a big, modern apartment in London and an expensive car and …

J: A Rolls-Royce or Bentley?

B: No, I'd rather have a sports car – an Aston Martin or a Porsche perhaps.

J: And what about work. Would you stop working?

B: Of course! It would be a full-time job spending all that money.

3
J: Excuse me, can I ask you what you'd like to do with all the money that's in the jackpot this week?

C: Of course, dear. Well, I wouldn't want to change a thing really. I'd give half of the money to my children and my sister and I'd like to give the other half to charity.

J: That's very generous. Which charity would you give it to?

C: I don't really know yet, dear, but I'd hate to give it to one of those charities where most of the money goes on administration.

16B, page 65, Exercise 4

I = Interviewer, **S** = Sam

I: So, tell me, what you would take with you to a desert island.

S: Erm … I'd take my mobile phone, some make-up, and … lots of pizzas.

I: But if you were on a desert island, a mobile phone wouldn't work. There wouldn't be a signal.

S: That doesn't matter. If there wasn't a signal, I'd just play games on it.

I: And why would you need make-up? You'd be alone on the island.

S: Ah, but if a ship rescued me, I'd want to look nice.

I: OK. And all the pizzas?

S: Simple. I love pizza.

16C, page 66, Exercise 3

A = Man, **B** = Woman

A: I'm not happy with our paper supplier. I think we should look for a new one.

B: What's the problem? We've used them for years and we've never had any trouble with them.

A: Well, I'm afraid I think their paper's too expensive.

B: Yes, but we've tried using cheaper paper and it jammed the photocopiers.

A: Yes, but we could try to find a cheaper supplier of the paper we use now.

B: No, I don't think we should. They've always been reliable.

A: Well, … maybe you're right, but I still think we should ask some other companies to send us offers.

B: Do you really think we'll find a better offer?

A: Yes, I think we will.

Answer key

Unit 1

A

Ex 1

	Country he/she is from	City he/she is living in at the moment	What he/she likes about the city they live in	What he/she doesn't like about the city they live in	Who he/she knows
Christof	Germany	New York	it's exciting and lively	the long working hours	Chandrika, Chun Hua
Chandrika	India	Vancouver	the friendly people	the weather	Jenny, Christof
Jenny	Australia	London	the shops	the weather	Chandrika
Chun Hua	China	Munich	it's clean	the food	Christof

Ex 2
1 is walking **2** is working
3 calls **4** is raining **5** phones
6 misses **7** is flying
8 is studying

Ex 3
1 Sam **likes** London.
2 **I'm listening** to you. Please continue.
3 New York **has** a lot of people.
4 I **drive** to London every weekend.
5 **Do you know** Samantha?
6 John**'s phoning** his mother right now so I can't ask him.
7 **Do you want** a cup of tea?
8 I **don't need** any help at the moment, thank you.

Ex 4
1 c **2** e **3** f **4** b **5** d **6** a

Ex 5
1 knows a lot of people
2 studying Maths
3 lose weight
4 drinks mineral water
5 make mistakes
6 belong to a professional organization

B

Ex 1
1 relationship **2** network
3 successful **4** contacts
5 benefits **6** acquaintances
7 socializing **8** people

Ex 2
1 We always eat fish on Friday.
2 What are you doing?
3 Does he work in London?
4 I normally check my emails every morning.
5 Do you usually send postcards?
6 What time does Silvia get up in the morning?
7 I attend two conferences every year.
8 I am studying English in Canada.

Ex 3
1
a John **sometimes** goes to conferences to get new business contacts.
b He doesn't **always** remember names.
2
a Americans **often** change jobs several times in a lifetime.
b They don't **normally** stay in the same town all their lives. / They **normally** don't stay in the same town all their lives.
3
a I **never** throw away business cards.
b I don't **usually** remember to put them in a box. / I **usually** don't remember to put them in a box.
4
a I **frequently** go to social events because it's important to stay in touch with contacts.
b I don't **normally** stay until the end of the event. / I **normally** don't stay until the end of the event.

Ex 4
1 usually **2** rarely **3** never
4 often **5** always
6 sometimes

C

Ex 1
1 b **2** e **3** d **4** c **5** a

Ex 2
1 c **2** f **3** b **4** a **5** d **6** e

Ex 3
a Y **b** N **c** Y **d** Y **e** N **f** N

Ex 4
1 Would you like a cup of coffee?
2 Do you mind helping me with this translation?
3 Could you tell me the way to the station?
4 Would you like to have dinner with me this evening?
5 May I carry your bags for you?
6 Do you mind if I go early today?

Ex 5
1 Sorry. I'm afraid I need it myself this evening.
2 Please help yourself.
3 No, not at all. Go ahead.
4 Feel free.
5 Not at all.
6 Sure. Here you are.

Ex 6
1 N **2** Y **3** Y **4** Y **5** Y **6** Y

D

Ex 1
a 3 **b** 2 **c** 5 **d** 1 **e** 6 **f** 4

Ex 2
1 Debbie and May can help each other.
2 Daniel and Edward can help each other.

Ex 3
1 swap **2** contact **3** busy
4 community **5** join in
6 relatives **7** seeking
8 childminder

Ex 4
1 're looking for **2** 'm trying
3 think **4** need **5** Do you want
6 like **7** want **8** don't eat

Unit 2

A

Ex 1
Conversation 1
1 F **2** T
Conversation 2
3 T **4** F
Conversation 3
5 F **6** F
Conversation 4
7 T **8** T

Ex 2
Conversation 1
C: Good morning, BRD Softlab. My name's Cathy. How can I help you?
R: Oh, hello. My name's Richard Willis. I'm **having problems** installing a program, Money-Wise.
C: Which version of Money-Wise do you use, Mr Willis?
R: The latest version, 8.0.
C: OK, Mr Willis. Just a moment. **I'll put** you **through** to technical support.
Conversation 2
C: Oh no! Not again.
K: What's the matter, Chris?
C: The computer's **frozen.** It's the **third** time this morning and the last time it happened I lost an hour's work.
K: Really? How annoying. I'm going to the IT department for a meeting in a minute so I**'ll ask** one of the technicians to **come** and **have** a look at your PC.

Ex 3
1 e **2** c **3** a **4** h **5** b **6** g **7** d
8 f

B

Ex 1
1 f **2** d **3** a **4** h **5** b **6** c **7** e
8 g

Ex 2
1 I **2** F **3** I **4** F **5** F **6** F
7 F **8** I
a F **b** I **c** I **d** I **e** I **f** F **g** F **h** I

Ex 3
1 s.trotter@mail.com
2 maria_sanchez@california-gardens.org
3 www.houseandhome.co.uk
4 www.blogs.ct.com/deartom
5 www.ctvgroup.com/news/latest.php
6 j.maier@mattison.au

Ex 4
1 I'm looking forward to
2 I'm waiting for
3 I'm looking forward to
4 I'm expecting to
5 I'm expecting to
6 I'm waiting for
7 I'm looking forward to
8 I'm waiting for

Ex 5
1 Hi **2** Dear **3** Thanks
4 Yours sincerely **5** Love
6 Dear Mr

C

Ex 1
1 F **2** F **3** T **4** T **5** T **6** F

Ex 2
1 b **2** d **3** b **4** c **5** d **6** a
7 c **8** a

Ex 3
1 sorry I'm late
2 could you repeat that
3 really must apologize
4 we can't come to
5 I'm sorry to bother you
6 Please send me the bill

D

Ex 1
1 Hotel **2** Airport **3** Station
4 Hotel **5** Taxi **6** Airport
7 Taxi **8** Station

Ex 2
1 Hi Giuseppe. It's Heinrich here.
2 Hello Heinrich. Where are you?
3 I'm still on the train, but I'll be at the station in 20 minutes.
4 OK, I'll come and pick you up.
5 Oh thanks, Giuseppe. That's very kind of you.
6 It's no trouble. I'll be in a red Mini.
7 OK. Looking forward to seeing you.
8 Looking forward to seeing you, too.

Ex 3

R	X	T	E	R	M	I	N	A	L	Q
Y	O	S	U	I	T	C	A	S	E	J
Z	F	O	J	T	R	A	I	N	T	T
P	T	W	M	X	Z	Q	X	A	P	K
L	F	Q	A	I	S	L	E	I	A	Z
A	X	L	L	I	T	S	E	R	S	V
N	H	L	I	E	T	C	R	P	S	M
E	I	O	K	G	E	E	N	O	P	E
B	W	C	T	R	H	B	R	R	O	N
D	I	N	N	E	R	T	A	T	R	U
T	S	I	N	G	L	E	X	G	T	X

Ex 4
1 envelope 2 guest 3 the card
4 passenger 5 platform
6 check in 7 ticket 8 duty free

Ex 5
1 receipt 2 platform
3 hand luggage 4 bill
5 duty free 6 presentation
7 boarding card 8 passenger

Unit 3

A

Ex 1
1 went 2 ran 3 sang 4 ate
5 drank 6 caught 7 left
8 watched 9 wrote
10 worked

Ex 2
1 was 2 were 3 was 4 was
5 were 6 was
7 wasn't 8 weren't

Ex 3
1 became 2 was 3 died 4 were
5 began 6 won 7 had
8 decided 9 was 10 sold

Ex 4
1 was 2 came
3 died, didn't stay, went, taught
4 married, had 5 came, gave
6 was, didn't have

B

Ex 1
1 Yes, he was. 2 No, he wasn't.
3 Yes, they were.
4 No, he didn't. 5 No, it wasn't.
6 Yes, they did.

Ex 2
1 Did you go to university?/ Yes, I did.
2 Were you a good student?/ No, I wasn't.
3 Did you pass your exams? / No, I didn't.
4 Was your first job interesting?/Yes, it was.
5 Did you earn much money?/ No, I didn't.
6 Were your colleagues nice?/ Yes, they were.

Ex 3
1 Where were you born?
2 When did you leave China?
3 Why did you leave?
4 What did you study?
5 How long did you stay in London?
6 How much money did you earn in your first job?

Ex 4
1 Where did you get the money?
2 How much money did you need?
3 Did you start the business alone?
4 How did you get the idea?
5 Did you have any problems?
6 What business contacts did you have?
7 Did you lose any money?
8 When did your company become a success?

Ex 5
1 **Did** people enjoy the party last night?
2 I didn't **go** to the party.
3 Did John **know** the answer?
4 He **caught** the plane on time.
5 **Did** the plane arrive on time yesterday?
6 We **went** on holiday last month.
7 **Was** it a good party last night?
8 **Were** Mike and Patty at school together?
9 Did Antje **see** the film yesterday?
10 They **found** the stolen car.

Ex 6
1 success 2 failed 3 successful
4 succeed 5 failure 6 success

C

Ex 1
B: How terrible!
B: You poor thing
2
B: That's great!, Congratulations!
B: Brilliant!
3
B: Wow! That's fantastic!
B: Oh no!, What a shame.
4
B: That's terrible.
B: What a nuisance.

Ex 2

Reacting to good news	Reacting to bad news
That's great!	How terrible!
Congratulations!	You poor thing.
Brilliant!	Oh no!
Wow!	What a shame.
That's fantastic!	That's terrible.
	What a nuisance.

Ex 3
1 c 2 h 3 f 4 a 5 b 6 e
7 g 8 d

Ex 4
1 That's terrible.
2 That's a pity.
3 That's a nuisance.
4 Wow!
5 That's a shame.
6 That's terrific.

Ex 5
1 How was your holiday?
2 Where did you go?
3 Was the weather good?
4 Was the food good?
5 Did you enjoy Rome?
6 Did you visit the Colosseum?

D

Ex 1
1 b 2 d 3 e 4 a 5 f 6 c

Ex 2
1 was 2 made 3 invented
4 tried 5 didn't stop 6 didn't fail
7 didn't work 8 learnt

Ex 3
1 c 2 a 3 f 4 b 5 e 6 d
7 h 8 g

Ex 4
1 spent a lot of money
2 improved efficiency
3 installed new machinery
4 ran tests
5 solved the problems
6 speeded up production
7 missed the deadline
8 achieved our targets

Ex 5
1 didn't get 2 wanted 3 missed
4 ran 5 didn't find 6 discovered
7 solved 8 caused

Unit 4

A

Ex 1
1 b 2 a 3 a 4 c

Ex 2
1 faster 2 more interesting
3 better 4 longer 5 more open
6 quicker

Ex 3
1 S 2 Q 3 Q 4 S 5 S 6 Q

B

Ex 1
1 smaller
2 the most experienced
3 less reliable 4 the happiest
5 more helpful 6 tidy
7 better 8 bad

Ex 2
1 most expensive 2 oldest
3 biggest 4 most important
5 best 6 most popular

Ex 3
1 worst 2 less expensive
3 funnier 4 better
5 most unusual
6 more beautiful, cheaper
7 best 8 most awful, ugliest

Ex 4
1 F – The Amazon River is the second longest river in the world. (Nile = 7,088 km, Amazon = 6,670 km).
2 F – Jeanne Calment (1875–1997), was 122 years and 164 days old when she died.
3 T – Texas = 695,622 km², Alaska = 1,717,854 km².
4 T – The tallest tree in the world is a Coastal Redwood in California. It is 115.56 m high.
5 F – The hottest land temperature ever recorded was 57.8° C in Al 'Aziziyah, Libya.
6 T

C

Ex 1
a 2 b 1 c 5 d 3 e 4

Ex 2
1
A: I **love** your new hair style. It **looks great**.
B: Thanks, I'm glad you like it.
A: Yes, short hair **really suits** you.
2
A: Here's a little something for all the help you've given us.
B: Oh, thank you, they're **beautiful**, but it really isn't **necessary**.
A: Don't be silly! You're **welcome**.
3
A: I **really like** your blog. It's full of useful information.
B: Oh, thanks. Sometimes I think my posts are a bit technical.
A: No, not **at all** – even I can understand them.
4
A: Oh no! I've forgotten the cable for the digital projector.
B: No **problem**. I've got one in my office. I'll get it.
A: Thanks, that's **brilliant**. You're a **lifesaver**.
5
A: Just let us know what you need from the shops and we'll get it for you.
B: Thanks Mary, but are you **sure**? I don't want you to go to any trouble.
A: Don't be **silly**. It's no **trouble**. It's only for a couple of weeks until you're well again.

Ex 3
1 much **2** gift **3** conference
4 appreciate **5** Thanks
6 lifesaver

Ex 4
1 a **2** c **3** b **4** a **5** b **6** c **7** b
8 c **9** b **10** a

D

Ex 1

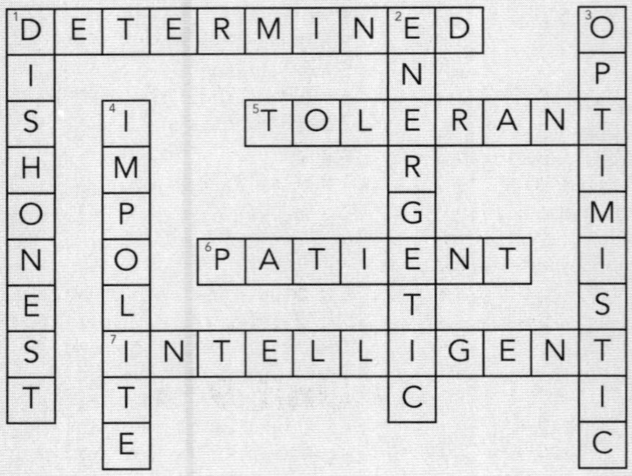

Ex 2
1 energetic **2** intelligent
3 optimistic **4** impolite
5 patient **6** dishonest
7 tolerant **8** determined

Ex 3
1 most important **2** more urgent
3 best **4** closer
5 more important **6** most urgent
7 least important

Unit 5

A

Ex 1
1 T **2** F **3** F **4** F **5** T **6** F

Ex 2
1 b **2** c **3** a

Ex 3
A
1 limit the meetings to one hour
3 hold meetings standing up
4 start on time
B
1 not send big attachments
2 have one file for all teams
4 stop printing everything
C
2 have one person to check all team and project work
3 share information with all teams
4 not have two teams working on the same project

Ex 4
1
A: How **are we going to solve** them?
B: We**'re going to hire** a consultant to help us.
2
A: When **are we going to tidy** it?
B: We**'re going to come** to work on Saturday and tidy it then.
3
A: What **are you going to do** about it? I need to send you the report.
B: **I'm going to delete** some emails this afternoon.
4
A: Oh no! **Are you going to buy** a new one?
B: Yes, but we**'re not/aren't going to spend** a lot of money.
5
A: Really? When **are you going to quit?**
B: As soon as I can. **I'm not going to do** another boring job again.
6
B: Oh, really? When **are you going to retire?**
A: Next year. **I'm going to travel** around the world.

B

Ex 1
1 It'll be cold and wet tomorrow.
2 Most people won't stop learning in the future.
3 There'll be more free time.
4 She'll learn Chinese.
5 I'll need to change my job several times.
6 We won't finish school before we're 18.

Ex 2
1 I'll contact **2** I'll fill in **3** I'll mail
4 I'll deal with **5** I'll delete
6 I won't to put it off
7 won't find **8** won't speak
9 I'll rearrange **10** I'll send

Ex 3
1
Will lifelong learning be important for everyone?
Yes, it will.
2
Will most people retire earlier?
No, they won't.
3
Will employees need more skills?
Yes, they will.
4
Will English be a second language for most people?
Yes, it will.
5
Will multi-tasking increase productivity?
No, it won't.
6
Will children spend less time at school?
No, they won't.

Ex 4
1 c **2** a **3** f **4** b **5** d **6** e

Ex 5
1 I want to learn a new language so **I'm going to study** Chinese next year.
2 Please email me the details and **I'll arrange** the meeting for you.
3 Harry **won't pass** his exams because he never studies.
4 **We're going to introduce** some changes that will increase productivity.
5 **I'm not going to pay off** my debts this month because I can't afford it.
6 The weather report said that it **won't rain** today so let's go to the beach!

C

Ex 1
1 Can you lend me $10?
2 Do you mind if I open the window?
3 Could you pick me up at 4 p.m.?
4 Would you get me a glass of water?
5 Can you give me a hand?
6 May I borrow your calculator?

Ex 2
1 b **2** d **3** e **4** a **5** f **6** c

Ex 3
1 g **2** b **3** a **4** d **5** j **6** h
7 i **8** f **9** c **10** e

Ex 4
1 I **2** I **3** I **4** D **5** I **6** I **7** D
8 I **9** D **10** D

Ex 5
1 D **2** I **3** I **4** D

Ex 6
1
A: Do you think I **could borrow** your car?
B: I'm **afraid** not …
A: No **problem**. I'll take the bus.
2
A: I've got my English test tomorrow and I can't find my **dictionary** anywhere.
B: **Do you want** to take mine?
A: That **would be** great.
3
A: **Would** you **like** to stay for dinner?
B: I don't want to be any **trouble**.
4
A: **Could** you **help** me with this email? I don't know what to write.
B: Yes, **of course**. Just give me a minute and I'll be right with you.

Ex 7
1 happy **2** How **3** OK **4** why
5 could **6** easiest

D

Ex 1
1 managing **2** waste **3** run
4 put off **5** efficiently
6 deal with

Ex 2
1 d **2** f **3** a **4** b **5** c **6** e

Ex 3
1 request **2** different **3** future
4 multitasking **5** difficult
6 hire **7** mess **8** accountant
9 put off
Hidden word: EFFICIENT

Unit 6

A

Ex 1
1 Length **2** 8.6 cm **3** Width
4 Weight **5** Six
6 Top/maximum speed
7 20 min **8** Price

Ex 2
1 c **2** b **3** b

Ex 3
1 two point one, eight, five
2 three quarters
3 five hundred thousand and fifty
4 fourteen euros ninety-five (cents)
5 two thousand one hundred and eighty-five
6 five hundred and fifty thousand
7 oh/zero, eight, nine, three, one, four, seven, nine, two, six, one
8 twelve million eight hundred and fifty thousand
9 nine hundred (and) sixty-seven point two, five, four
10 oh/zero, eight, double five (five, five), one, four, treble one (one, one, one), seven, nine

B

Ex 1
1 heavy **2** height **3** width
4 long **5** depth **6** fast

Ex 2
1 F **2** F **3** T **4** T **5** T, **6** F

Ex 3
1 How long is it? / What's the length?
2 How wide is it? / What's the width?
3 How much does it weigh? / What's the weight (of the car)?
4 How fast can it go? / What's the top speed (of the car)?
5 How powerful is the electric engine? / How much power can the electric engine produce?
6 How much is it? / How much does it cost? / What does it cost?

Ex 4
1 83 mm **2** 44 mm **3** 190 grams
4 over five million **5** No
6 £249

C

Ex 1
1 b **2** c **3** a **4** a **5** c **6** b

Ex 2
1 e **2** b **3** d **4** f **5** a **6** c

Ex 3
d e

Ex 4
A Good afternoon, madam. Can I help you?
B Yes, I'd like to know a **bit more about** the red car out there.
A Ah, The Golf? Well, it's only had one careful **owner** and no **accidents**.
B Yes, it looks as if it's in very good **condition**.
A Yes, there's nothing wrong with that car. I'm **offering** it with a two-year guarantee.
B Really?
A Yes, there's been a lot of interest in that car, so if you're thinking of buying it, don't think too long because I **can't guarantee** that it'll still be for sale tomorrow.
B OK and you want £12,000 for it?

D

Ex 1
1 comfortable **2** harmful
3 reliable **4** wonderful, beautiful
5 fashionable **6** affordable

Ex 2
1 F **2** B **3** B **4** F **5** B **6** F
7 B **8** B **9** F **10** B

Ex 3
1 C **2** B **3** A **4** E **5** D

Unit 7

A

Ex 1
1 c **2** d **3** e **4** b **5** a **6** f

Ex 2
1 must **2** mustn't **3** mustn't
4 don't need to **5** should
6 have to **7** must **8** have to

Ex 3
1 F **2** T **3** T **4** F **5** F **6** T
7 T **8** F

Ex 4
1 improve **2** relax **3** morale
4 introduce **5** rules **6** casual
7 stress **8** difficult **9** everyone
10 benefit
Hidden word: PRODUCTIVE

B

Ex 1
1 d **2** e **3** c **4** a **5** f **6** b

Ex 2
1 Can you wear jeans at work?
2 Do you have to be at work before 9 a.m.?
3 Do I have to send the report today?
4 Do I need to ask for permission?
5 Should we switch off our mobile phones in meetings?
6 Can you make private calls in the office?

Ex 3
1 Can, can't **2** Do, don't
3 have, don't
4 Should, shouldn't
5 Do, don't **6** Can, can

Ex 4
1 casual **2** guidelines
3 employees **4** morale
5 increase **6** encourages
7 ideas **8** challenging

C

Ex 1
a 5 **b** 1 c 4 **d** 2 **e** 3

Ex 2
1 should **2** After that
3 Make sure **4** That's right
5 Next, should **6** don't forget

Ex 3
1 save **2** password **3** click
4 zoom in **5** paste **6** select
7 delete **8** print

Ex 4
1 H **2** U **3** H

Ex 5
1
1 Try not **2** need to **3** Next
4 everything clear
2
1 Save **2** Delete **3** Don't forget
4 Let's go
3
1 First **2** Exactly, Good
3 Good question **4** Don't forget

D

Ex 1
1 c **2** a **3** f **4** e **5** b **6** d

Ex 2
1 create a level playing field
2 throw in the towel
3 time out
4 give it your best shot
5 calls the shots
6 get off the hook

Ex 3
1 can **2** have to **3** need to
4 can't **5** have to **6** can
7 need to **8** must

Ex 4
1 c **2** d **3** b **4** e **5** a

Unit 8

A

Ex 1
1 T **2** F **3** F **4** T **5** T **6** F

Ex 2
1 have included **2** Have, thought
3 didn't think **4** Has, had
5 She's, using **6** hasn't, read

Ex 3
1 've updated **2** haven't read
3 Have, made **4** has, decided
5 have forgotten **6** has had
7 Has, changed **8** hasn't worked

Ex 4
1 Have you tried calling the hotline?
2 Have you ordered some more paper?
3 Have you updated the files?
4 Has Sarah sent us the parts we need?
5 Has the service engineer finished repairing the photocopier?
6 Have they sent the manual?

B

Ex 1
1 has already happened
2 hasn't happened yet
3 has already happened (Male 77.8 years, female 80.05)
4 has already happened (A Japanese magnetic levitation train – Maglev – reached a top speed of 581km/h (361 mph).
5 has already happened
6 has already happened (The first colour photographs were taken in 1907).
7 hasn't happened yet
8 has already happened

Ex 2
1 already **2** yet **3** already **4** yet
5 already **6** yet **7** yet
8 already, yet

Ex 3
1 Have you read the user manual already?/Have you already read the user manual?
2 Have you taken any photos with your new camera yet?
3 Have you used the navigation system yet?
4 Have you used that function yet?
5 Has the meeting finished already?/Has the meeting already finished?
6 Have you already installed the new software?/Have you installed the new software already?

Ex 4
1 He's already changed the £500 to euros.
2 He hasn't phoned Sally about the party yet.
3 He hasn't bought Maria a birthday present yet.
4 He's already made an appointment with Dr Peters.
5 He hasn't collected Steve yet.
6 He's already sent the report to Jenny.
7 He's already reserved a table at Bella Italia.
8 He hasn't renewed his passport yet.

C

Ex 1
1 I suggest going to bed earlier.
2 I recommend coming by train.
3 Why don't we give it to charity?
4 How about opening it in Krakow?
5 I suggest taking a taxi.
6 We could reduce the price.

Ex 2
1 d **2** a **3** f **4** b **5** c **6** e

Ex 3
1 T **2** F **3** T **4** F **5** T **6** T

D

Ex 1
1 f **2** e **3** d **4** b **5** c **6** a

Ex 2
1 a great idea / a brilliant idea
2 a crazy idea / a ridiculous idea
3 a new idea / an original idea
4 reject an idea / dismiss an idea
5 think about an idea / consider an idea
6 think of an idea / come up with an idea

Ex 3
1 d **2** a **3** b **4** c

Ex 4
c

Ex 5
1 b **2** c **3** a

Unit 9

A

Ex 1
1 will **2** Could **3** may not **4** will
5 might

Ex 2
1 predict **2** double **3** busy
4 keep in touch **5** events
6 spread

Ex 3
1 Could I help you instead?
2 Might John know some of the information?
3 May I have a look at the list?
4 Will you help us?
5 Might I ask a quick question?
6 Could you stay later this evening?

Ex 4
1 mightn't **2** Could **3** will
4 may not **5** won't **6** Could

B

Ex 1
1 is building **2** 'm scheduling
3 're inviting **4** 're attending
5 'm meeting **6** 's arriving

Ex 2
1 What time are you arriving at the airport?
2 How are you getting to the hotel?
3 Where are you staying?
4 Who are you meeting?
5 Why are you meeting her?
6 How long are you staying?

Ex 3
1 We're meeting our London colleagues next Monday.
2 Alan is going on a business trip in April.
3 Ryan isn't going to the party next Saturday.
4 Is Claire organizing the next conference?
5 Patrick isn't flying to the meeting in March.
6 Are you travelling to India next week?

Ex 4
1 Frank **2** New York **3** John
4 Mike's office **5** six o'clock

Ex 5
1 'm travelling **2** 're having
3 urgently **4** 're meeting
5 're going **6** appointments
7 're driving **8** interview

C

Ex 1
1 A **2** P **3** R **4** N **5** I **6** A
7 N **8** N **9** P **10** A **11** R
12 A

Ex 2
1
a 4 **b** 1 **c** 6 **d** 2 **e** 5 **f** 3
2
a 5 **b** 1 **c** 2 **d** 4 **e** 3

Ex 3
1 b **2** c **3** a **4** e **5** d

Ex 4
1 H **2** A **3** R

Ex 5
1 doing anything special
2 really **3** Would you like
4 great **5** get back
6 let me know **7** got any plans
8 going on **9** having **10** make it
11 love to come
12 Would you like
13 afraid 14 No problem

D

Ex 1
1 give, message **2** give, time
3 gave, talk **4** give, smile
5 give, reason **6** give, advice

Ex 2
a 2 **b** 5 **c** 1 **d** 4 **e** 3 **f** 6

Ex 3
1 birthday party
2 house warming party
3 Halloween party
4 dinner party
5 fancy dress party?
6 retirement party

Ex 4
1 invitation **2** diary **3** attending
4 get-together **5** schedule
6 may **7** apologize

Ex 5
1 scheduling **2** surprise
3 late **4** refuse **5** charity
Hidden word: DIARY

Unit 10

A

Ex 1
1 1,200 **2** 200 **3** £39 **4** £28,000

Ex 2
1 U **2** C **3** C **4** C **5** C **6** U
7 U **8** C **9** U **10** C **11** C **12** U

Ex 3
1 How many **2** How many
3 How much **4** How many
5 How much **6** How many
7 How many **8** How much

Ex 4
1 There are a lot of
2 There isn't much
3 There aren't any
4 Is there a lot
5 Are there many
6 There isn't any

Ex 5
1 there isn't any
2 Are there many
3 there are a lot of
4 Are there any
5 are there any
6 there are a lot of

B

Ex 1
1 F **2** T **3** T **4** F **5** F **6** T

Ex 2
1
1 not very **2** too far
3 too dangerous **4** terrible
5 too hot **6** cool down enough
7 too expensive **8** good enough

Ex 3
1 is too much **2** are too many
3 is too **4** are too **5** is too
6 are too many

Ex 4
1 I don't think we'll have **enough** time to visit the museum today.
2 The hotel isn't really central **enough**.
3 Do we have **enough** money to buy the tickets or do I need to change some?
4 It's 80 km around the lake and that's long **enough** for my first bike ride this year.
5 Do you think the weather will be warm **enough** to go camping there in March?
6 We wanted to go skiing, but there wasn't **enough** snow.

Ex 5
1 These jeans are too expensive
2 I don't have enough money
3 It is very hot in here
4 There wasn't enough hot water for a shower this morning
5 There were too many people in the pool
6 There wasn't enough space on the bus

C

Ex 1
1 T **2** T **3** F **4** T **5** F **6** F

Ex 2
1 b **2** a **3** b **4** c **5** a **6** c

D

Ex 1
1 A **2** C **3** B

Ex 2
1 No, the city was built in 1956.
2 Yes
3 Yes, it is one of the oldest cities in the world.
4 Yes, it does.
5 No, it's not. It is the fourth biggest.
6 Yes

Ex 3
1 d **2** e **3** f **4** b **5** a **6** c

Unit 11

A

Ex 1
1 d **2** f **3** a **4** g **5** b **6** h
7 c **8** e

Ex 2
1 not worth repairing
2 worth paying
3 is worth
4 worth seeing
5 is it worth
6 be worth
7 worth asking
8 not worth working

Ex 3
1 works, 'll collapse
2 feels, goes
3 takes, doesn't relax/won't relax
4 isn't, 'll look
5 change, won't get
6 Will you be, get

B

Ex 1
1 When **2** When **3** If **4** if **5** If
6 when **7** If **8** when

Ex 2
1 c; if **2** h; if **3** f; when **4** d; if
5 b; if **6** g; when **7** a; if
8 e; when

Ex 3
1 'll ask **2** won't start **3** went
4 'll be **5** don't leave
6 won't repair **7** won't sign
8 'll be waiting

Ex 4
1 c **2** a **3** e **4** b **5** f **6** d

C

Ex 1
1 chain **2** secret **3** habits
4 public **5** branches **6** re-install
7 theft **8** permission

Ex 2
1 T **2** F **3** F **4** F **5** F **6** T

Ex 3
1 staff **2** theft **3** could hire
4 worth **5** security guards
6 but they're expensive
7 why don't we **8** search

Ex 4
1 A **2** A **3** D **4** A **5** D

Ex 5
1 e **2** a **3** f **4** d **5** b **6** c

D

Ex 1
1 don't **2** don't need
3 will help **4** are not used to
5 will be **6** have

Ex 2
1 If **2** When **3** When **4** If
5 When **6** If/When

Ex 3
1 c **2** e **3** b **4** f **5** c **6** a

Ex 4
1 We're planning to **install** exercise **machines** in the staff restroom to help employees keep fit.
2 Can I **give** you some **advice**? Don't resign from your job.
3 We **set up an experiment** to find out which jobs require the most walking.
4 I'm going to completely **change** my **lifestyle** starting today. I want to be fitter and healthier.
5 I'd rather have an interesting job than **earn** a lot of **money**.
6 You don't look very well. You need to **do** more **exercise**. Start by taking the stairs not the lift every day.

Unit 12

A

Ex 1
1 F **2** F **3** T **4** T **5** T

Ex 2
1 A **2** P **3** P **4** A **5** P **6** A

Ex 3
1 was released **2** were filmed
3 is often described
4 is based on **5** was shot
6 is ranked as

Ex 4
1 e **2** b **3** c **4** h **5** f **6** a **7** g
8 d

B

Ex 1
1 A **2** B **3** B **4** B **5** A **6** A
7 B **8** A

Ex 2
Active: 2, 3, 5
Passive: 1, 4, 7, 8
Both: 6

Ex 3
1 seats **2** is reserved
3 are grown **4** cook
5 is served **6** are homemade
7 speak **8** do not accept

Ex 4

places to eat	meat	vegetables	staff	parts of a meal
café	beef	beans	chef	dessert
canteen	chicken	carrots	cook	main course
diner	duck	cauliflower	manager	side dish
restaurant	lamb	peas	waiter	soup
snack bar	pork	potatoes	waitress	starter

Ex 5

1 waiter **2** starter **3** main course
4 canteen/restaurant
5 snack bar/diner **6** chef/cook

C

Ex 1

1 C 2 A 3 B

Ex 2

1 Have you skied before?
2 When did Tim learn to ski?
3 Is he a good skier?

Ex 3

A: We're going skiing in Switzerland next month. We've booked a room at a guest house in the canton of Valais.
B: Ah yes, that is a very nice area for skiing. My husband, Klaus, and I went skiing there several times before we got married.
C: The skiing conditions are usually very good there in March. Are you staying near Verbier?
A: Yes, we're staying in Bagnes. Do you know it?
C: Yes, I know it very well. It's in the valley. It's only a ten-minute drive from Verbier.
A: I see you are both experts on the area. Can you recommend any restaurants there?
B: Yes, there was a very good one, but I'm afraid I can't remember the name of it now. I'll have to ask Klaus.

Ex 4

They develop the conversation by asking questions.

Ex 5

A: I'm going skiing next month.
E: **Have you been skiing before?/ Have you ever been skiing before?**
A: No, it's the first time.
E: **Where are you going?**
A: Zermatt in Switzerland.
E: Oh, it's wonderful there. **Are you staying in a hotel?/Have you booked a hotel?**
A: Yes, we're staying in a lovely hotel right in the town centre.
B: **How long are you staying?**
A: Just ten days. We'd like to stay longer, but Chris has to be back at work on the 7th.

D

Ex 1

The Festival of San Fermin
The festival of San Fermin takes place in the old part of Pamplona, Spain from 6th – 14th July every year. Its most famous event is The Running of the Bulls. The festival dates back to the thirteenth century but the 825-metre route that is run today began when the bullring was built in 1844. The run begins at 8:00 a.m. when a rocket is lit. It is a dangerous festival: since 1924, 14 people have been killed and over 200 have been badly injured. The organizers hand out information (with safety tips) before the event. When the bulls have entered the ring, young cows are then released into the arena.

The Lantern Festival
The Lantern Festival takes place on the fifteenth day of the first month of the Chinese calendar. Emperor Wudi of the Han Dynasty declared it as one of the most important festivals in 104 BC. During the festival children go out at night with paper lanterns. The night is full of bright colours and lights. Some of the lanterns have riddles inside them which can be pulled out and read. If the reader knows the answer, they win a little prize. Another important part of the festival is eating sweet rice dumplings called *Yuan Xiao*. Each area has its own special way of making them.

Ex 2

1 is held **2** are painted **3** decide
4 is played **5** play **6** dances

Unit 13

A

Ex 1

1 b 2 c 3 c 4 a 5 c 6 b

Ex 2

1 an **interesting** new idea, **amazing** ideas
2 **giving** people so little time means some people may not be able to come, **Holding** meetings in the afternoon is always a good idea, **Writing** the email in the meeting would be rude.
3 Some people **like leaving** their mobile phones on in meetings, Invite everyone to chat for five minutes, e.g. about the weather, what they **enjoy doing**, their holiday plans, etc.

Ex 3

1 arriving **2** talking **3** inviting
4 mixing **5** giving **6** seeing

B

Ex 1

1 T 2 T 3 F 4 T 5 F 6 T

Ex 2

1 surprised, relaxed
2 insulted, interesting
3 shocked, surprised

Ex 3

1 B 2 C 3 A

Ex 4

1 interested **2** boring
3 embarrassed **4** disappointing
5 exhausted **6** concentrating

C

Ex 1

1 T 2 F 3 T 4 T 5 T 6 F

Ex 2

1 e 2 c 3 f 4 a 5 d 6 b

Ex 3

1 brilliant **2** look **3** suits
4 wonderful **5** beautiful
6 fantastic, talented **7** really nice
8 absolutely delicious

D

Ex 1

1 a 2 a 3 b 4 c 5 a 6 c

Ex 2

1 G 2 H 3 H 4 B 5 G 6 G
7 H 8 B

Ex 3

1 d 2 e 3 a 4 h 5 b 6 g 7 f
8 c

Unit 14

A

Ex 1

1 T 2 F 3 T 4 T 5 F 6 T

Ex 2

1 left **2** was **3** started **4** bought
5 set up **6** married **7** has starred
8 have been **9** has been
10 has, become

B

Ex 1

1 No they haven't. (They haven't seen each other for years).
2 He works for a company called SoftX.
3 He has been with SoftX for about ten years.
4 Sue has been with Patchwork Communications since she married Carlos and they moved to San Diego.
5 Carlos has had his company for five years.
6 He lost a major client last year.

Ex 2

1 haven't seen **2** left **3** 've been
4 since **5** five years ago
6 lost

Ex 3

1 for **2** since **3** for **4** since **5** for
6 for **7** since **8** for

Ex 4

1 I have wanted to go to New Zealand ~~for~~ **since** I saw a documentary about it.
2 I ~~have been~~ **went** to university from 2002 – 2005.
3 We have lived in this house ~~since~~ **for** five years.
4 I ~~have~~ **had** my first car for five years and then bought a motorbike.
5 Have you ever ~~went~~ bold to Canada?
6 Tom ~~is~~ **has been** working here for about six months.

Ex 5

1 Harry has been working for Texas Instruments since 1999.
2 Greg and Janet have been married since 2003.
3 Beatrice lived in Stockholm for six years.
4 Ali has just read *The Lord of the Rings*.

C

Ex 1

1 No, some cultures think this is unnecessary or even rude.
2 Native speakers often speak too quickly and unclearly and use difficult language.
3 Experts sometimes forget that some people may not understand the specialized words they use.
4 If you watch your audience carefully you can see when you have said something that is not clear to them and can stop and make the point easier to understand.
5 No, American audiences are more interested in the big picture and what the bottom line is.
6 No, in some cultures people bang their hands on the table to say thank you to the speaker.

Ex 2

1 T 2 F 3 T 4 F 5 F

Ex 3

1 d 2 a 3 f 4 e 5 c 6 b 7 h
8 g

D

Ex 1

P	R	O	J	E	C	T	V	S	M
Q	X	T	E	A	M	K	L	Q	A
J	C	R	W	S	Z	L	Y	U	N
Q	I	O	U	Y	I	L	S	A	A
F	J	N	M	K	P	Q	A	L	G
B	O	S	S	P	H	X	L	I	E
B	B	Q	A	Z	A	I	A	F	R
O	F	F	I	C	E	N	R	I	X
Z	X	E	M	P	L	O	Y	E	R
P	O	S	I	T	I	O	N	D	Y

Ex 2
1 b **2** c **3** b **4** a **5** c **6** b **7** c
8 a

Ex 3
1 S **2** P **3** P **4** S **5** P **6** P **7** S
and P **8** S

Ex 4
1 c **2** e **3** a **4** f **5** b **6** d

Ex 5
1 C **2** A **3** B

Unit 15

A

Ex 1
1 F **2** F **3** F **4** F **5** F **6** F

Ex 2
1 was skiing
2 was studying
3 was having
4 was probably driving
5 wasn't raining
6 wasn't sleeping, was having

B

Ex 1
1 c **2** d **3** f **4** e **5** a **6** b

Ex 2
1 b **2** a **3** f **4** e **5** c **6** d

Ex 3
1 was driving, heard
2 met, was staying
3 broke, were skiing
4 was doing, was sleeping/was asleep
5 was walking, slipped, fell
6 crashed, was writing
7 was having, broke into, stole
8 went off, was

Ex 4
1 See you at eight.
2 Are you coming later?
3 Here's a question for you.
4 OK, great! See you tomorrow.
5 Is anyone going to Jake's tonight?/Anyone going to Jake's tonight?
6 I see you are at work.
7 Please call me before you come.
8 Thanks for letting me know. Will you be late?

Ex 5
a 5 **b** 3 **c** 8 **d** 1 **e** 6 **f** 7 **g** 2
h 4

C

Ex 1
1 reminding **2** left **3** remember
4 remind **5** forgot **6** left

Ex 2
1 remind **2** left **3** remember
4 leave **5** forgotten **6** reminded
7 remember **8** forget, left

Ex 3
1 d **2** a **3** f **4** b **5** c **6** e

Ex 4
1 b **2** a **3** d, e **4** c, f

Ex 5
1 I'm sorry that I forgot to call you yesterday but it was a really busy day.
2 I'm sorry I've kept you waiting. The meeting took longer than I thought it would.
3 I'm afraid I left the presentation in my office but I'll call Tom and ask him to email it.
4 I'm afraid I won't be able to come on Saturday. I forgot we're visiting Anne's parents.
5 I'm sorry but you'll have to remind me of your name. I can never remember names.
6 Oh, I am terribly sorry, I thought it was my coffee. Let me buy you another one.

Ex 6
1 d **2** c **3** f **4** a **5** b **6** e

D

Ex 1
1 b **2** c **3** a

Ex 2
1 F **2** F **3** T **4** F **5** T **6** T

Ex 3
1 did you do **2** had
3 dancing **4** went
5 was still trying **6** didn't notice

Unit 16

A

Ex 1
1 F **2** T **3** T **4** T **5** F **6** T **7** F
8 T **9** F

Ex 2
Interview 1
1 would you do
2 I'd like to travel, I'd love to do
Interview 2
3 you'd like to do
4 I'd rather have
Interview 3
5 wouldn't want to change
6 I'd hate to

Ex 3
1 'd like
2 Would you prefer to
3 'd rather have
4 'd hate to
5 'd rather not
6 wouldn't want to
7 Would ... be possible
8 'd love to

B

Ex 1
a I would talk to a lawyer
b If you took the money
c if one of your colleagues refused to accept the cut

Ex 2
1 c **2** a **3** b

Ex 3
1 F **2** F **3** F **4** T **5** T **6** F

Ex 4
1 take **2** take **3** were **4** work
5 wasn't **6** play **7** need **8** be
9 rescued **10** want

C

Ex 1
1 tell **2** say **3** telling **4** say **5** tell
6 telling

Ex 2
1 said **2** tell **3** say **4** told **5** tell
6 say

Ex 3
A: I'm not happy with our paper supplier. I think we should look for a new one.
B: What's the problem? We've used them for years and we've never had any trouble with them.
A: Well, I'm afraid I think their paper's too expensive.
B: Yes, but we've tried using cheaper paper and it jammed the photocopiers.
A: Yes, but we could try to find a cheaper supplier of the paper we use now.
B: No, I don't think we should. They've always been reliable.
A: Well, … maybe you're right but I still think we should ask some other companies to send us offers.
B: Do you really think we'll find a better offer?
A: Yes, I think we will.

Ex 4
1 d **2** a **3** e **4** c **5** f **6** b

D

Ex 1

1 S	U	2 R	V	I	V	E	3 D				4 S	
		E					I		5 H		A	
6 R	I	S	K				E		A		F	
		C					7 D	A	N	G	E	R
	8 P	U	B	9 L	I	C			G			
		E		I			10 C	L	I	F	F	
				F					N			
	11 S	A	V	E	D		12 A	N	G	R	Y	

Ex 2
1 c (Ice can be used like a magnifying glass to focus the sun's rays and produce enough heat to start a fire.)
2 b (You can live for longer than three days without a knife or food, but most people would die if they didn't drink for more than three days.)
3 b (The average person would die after three weeks of having nothing to eat.)
4 a (Experts say that your chances of survival are higher if you stay near the plane. A plane that has crashed can be seen from the air much better than a person on foot.)
5 c (A lot of fruit, berries and plants are poisonous, so unless you are a botanist/expert, it is safer to eat insects. Be careful though, some insects can be poisonous, especially brightly coloured ones.)
6 a (A bear can run much faster then you can, so forget about running away. Some people say that a bear won't attack you if you pretend to be dead but if the bear is hungry, it would have no problem eating you.)